GOD'S UNIVERSE, GOD'S RULES

JERRY MITCHELL

Ordering Information:

Books to Life Marketing Ltd
128 City Road, London, EC1V 2NX, UK

Printed in the United States of America

CHAPTER 1

WHEN WE CONSIDER our Bibles to be the instruction manuals for our lives and for each aspect of humanity, we should find a consistent theme from beginning to end. Psalm 33:4 tells us the word of the Lord is right and true and Proverbs 30:5 reads that every word of God is flawless, true, tested or proven depending on the translation we read. So how can God's words be true and right if they contain contradictions? Several books have already been written about the inconsistencies and contradictions contained in Scripture, some exploit those "apparent contradictions" while others fail to satisfactorily resolve those contradictions. While I can't satisfy everyone's questions, I can strive to search through the language, the culture and the history to discover where some of these so called contradictions are and why we think of them as not being consistent.

I will freely admit that I am examining the Bible from the viewpoint that it must be true and right just as King David wrote so many years ago. Because for David and Solomon to be right there should be no contradictions in the word of our God but consistent teaching from beginning to end. We shouldn't need to justify God's word if it is indeed perfect. It should be able to stand on it's own merit without the need for our adding to it or subtracting from it. This viewpoint allows us to hold our traditions and doctrines to the authority of the Scripture, not holding the Bible accountable to what we think it should tell us. Too often in our modern and enlightened world we consider science or some other theology as the standard to test the Bible: instead I will use the Bible as the only standard to test all of the other ideas that have crept into our modern way of thinking.

Our culture reflects the way we choose to treat our relationship with God. Most Christians today concentrate on getting into Heaven and while that is admirable, it is destination oriented. Our modern western culture has people searching out the cheapest and fasted way to reach our destinations; whether it is work, school, vacation or some other place we do our best to get there as fast as we can and as cheaply as we can. Unfortunately we treat reaching our eternity the same way; what is the least I need to do and still get into Heaven and have that wonderful personal relationship with God and our Savior? The Bible doesn't concentrate on a cheap or quick trip to anywhere, the Bible has a focus on the journey. The way we interact with others and with our Creator is the primary and consistent teaching from Genesis through Revelation. The people we encounter on the pages of scripture are real people, living real lives in very real circumstances. The lessons we are to learn from them are extremely important; so important in fact that many of those lessons are repeated quite often and yet we diminish their importance by calling them stories and not lessons.

When we try to compare the Bible to our new ideas or force the Bible to accept our concept of we think it should say, we are undermining biblical Authority. By holding our concepts and ideas up the the biblical standard, we acknowledge that the Bible is our supreme Authority. Within our culture today are many differing ideas about God, the origin of the universe, how we should treat each other, where and how we spend eternity and a myriad of other things all of which are tempting us away from the Bible. Evolutionists try to convince us that an explosion of nothing from nothing caused the universe to form and life came from nothing with no purpose. Atheists consider the world without God while other religions bombard us with their propaganda, each one proclaiming that they have the answers to all of our questions concerning who we are and what we are doing on this planet we call Earth. For Christians and Jewish believers alike Genesis should be our foundation and our starting point. For the jewish people Genesis not only reveals creation but the beginning of a wonderful group of people chosen by God to be His example of how we should live in this world. Sadly, Jews and Christians try to compromise the creation of the universe by adding millions of years to a six day creation described in the Bible. Believe it or not this is a much larger problem for Christians who believe the New Testament. In Isaiah 46 God proclaims the He has told us the end from the beginning.

How then I can it be possible for eschatological Christians (who are focused on the end times and getting into Heaven) to have any hope of understanding Revelation when they don't believe Genesis?

God tells us that He has shown us what will happen in Genesis. Jesus (Y'shua, his Hebrew name which I will use for the rest of this book out of respect for his given name) consistently refers to Genesis more than any other book in the Bible. One of the most quoted Bible verses in the world today is John 3:16 and is actually part of Y'shua chastising Nicodemus for not understanding Genesis. Many of the prophets refer to Genesis as well as the New Testament writers. With so many references to the first book of the Bible why and how are we able to dismiss believing what it reveals? Because we have turned the tables on Biblical Authority, trying to hold the Bible up to man's ideas and concepts instead of holding man's ideas to the Biblical standard.

For we as mere humans to think of ourselves being able to explain the origin of the universe better than the one who created it is ludicrous and even laughable but there are some who do just that. Many states support and have paleontology departments working with taxpayer dollars to convince people of millions of years of evolution. The museums we visit have signs proudly proclaiming that the dinosaurs went extinct 65 million years ago but the Bible tells us something completely different. Contained in the pages of our Bibles is a consistent lesson for us if we are willing to learn it. This lesson tells us that a supreme God, a God above all other gods created this universe and continues to run it according to His master plan. So why all of the confusion and doubt? Because we allow ourselves to get caught up with the modern ideas that "must" be right because science has a theory that proves it's own results. Again we fail to use the Bible as our standard by which we test man's ideas.

The eruption of Mount Saint Helens in 1980 has offered new insight to scientists about many things. We now know fossils can be produced in just a few weeks, there is no need for millions of years to form a fossil. The topography of the Mount Saint Helens area offers answers to the Grand Canyon formation and the vertical forest of fossilized trees. Immediately after the eruption scientist flocked to the volcano to observe in real time what they thought would take a millennium to recover. Surprised by their discoveries, very few secular scientists remained long term but the creation scientists continue to find biblical explanations and parallels between creation and the mount Saint Helens eruption. Many secular scientists wanted to compare the volcano to an end of the world scenario but were dismayed when they found an understanding of creation and scientific reasoning for the flood of Noah as well.

I'm sure you have heard about carbon dating or some other radioactive means of dating rocks, but what about collagen dating? Collagen is a connecting protein that is found throughout our body. Best described as "the stuff that holds us together" it is responsible for keeping our skin together as well as other jobs. Collagen breaks down reasonably quickly and according to most of the available research the longest collagen is able to remain in trace amounts under the best conditions is 100,000 years. When we consider this 100,000 year timeline and compare that to finding collagen in dinosaur bones which secular scientists tell us went extinct 65 million years ago; the math and science don't match. The Bible on the other hand does match with what we are able to observe in nature and in art and writings of our past and the archeology. In fact each time there is a "new" discovery, we find more convincing evidence that the Bible has been reliable when science fails.

Dinosaurs are fascinating, we seem to be so intrigued by that we allow our biblical standard and authority to fade away when they are mentioned. Nothing strikes fear in the hearts of Sunday School teachers more than when a child asks the question; "Were dinosaurs on Noah's ark?" when we use the Bible as our starting point and hold to Biblical Authority then the answer is yes. Of course we can also look to cave drawings and to asian temple art along with the writing from around the world to learn that dinosaurs as we know them today were indeed on the ark. There are many, many examples of archeological evidence which places humans right beside dinosaurs but when we look at the Bible we can't find the word dinosaur at all but we do find the word dragon. When we look at the book of Job we get a vivid description of what very well could be a fire breathing dragon, Job probably had some first hand knowledge to pass along about those large animals that were sharing this world just after Noah's flood. When we think about dinosaurs, our minds conjure up images of huge reptiles, larger than most houses thanks to our entertainment industry. the problem is most of what we call dinosaurs were not that big and the largest egg ever discovered is about the size of a football so for a reptile to get to be the size of what we consider a dinosaur it needed to live for about 1,000 years. There is much more about this topic to discuss but I will leave that to the dragon experts and continue with Biblical Authority.

Are you getting the idea that believing Genesis should be important to you? Allowing others to pull the wool over your eyes about evolution, science or theology is something that most of us learned as a result of being taught to compromise our position. After all how could the Bible be right when science has proven something but science hasn't proven the big bang, millions of years or evolution they are only secular theories. Christian and Jewish leaders should have fought tooth and nail beside each other to hold on to the Biblical account of creation but they were too busy fighting each other. Christian schools unfortunately either teach evolution or ignore creation completely. Jewish scientists include phrases in their writings such as "10,000 years ago" surely they should know better. Compromise has crumbled the Biblical foundation of Genesis, thankfully Biblical Authority can restore that foundation. Beginning with a firm foundation in Genesis we can look for the answers to practically every question in the world and expect to find an answer. God created more than what we can see, feel, hear, taste and smell, He created mathematics which helps us explain things like gravity. God created the abstract concepts we try to understand as well, music and art are as much a part of creation as Adam and Eve.

The lessons we learn in Genesis are consistent throughout the entire Bible and they are consistent in our universe today. Gravity works the same today as it did when God spoke and things began to form, the laws of physics haven't changed since before day one of creation either. Malachi 3:6 informs us that God does not change so that the sons of Jacob are not destroyed. If God decided to change the rules of gravity for instance what would be the consequences? What about math? do our numbers evolve? No, they remain constant because God remains constant. Our Creator's consistency in our physical world, doesn't change and it doesn't change in our spiritual world either. What God's plans were before creation remain intact. Our actions may have a minor impact on God's plans but don't think if we do or don't do something it will cause the world to end, just because God loves us doesn't mean we are so important that He will approve of whatever we do.

Remember the lesson we learn from Eve, the very first transcript of a conversation in the Bible is the serpent speaking to Eve. Everything was fine until she decided to add to the instructions concerning the fruit. The serpent knew exactly what God had told them about the fruit, quite simply don't eat it but apparently Eve thought she could improve on the word of God and she added "We shouldn't even touch it." That didn't work out vey well for Eve or the rest of us either and still here we are a few thousand years later and what are we doing? adding to or taking away from the word of God instead of allowing it to stand on it own merit. When we read about Eve or Cain or any of the other people throughout the Bible we learn that it is our actions more than our words which display our relationship to God. From the disobedience of Adam and Eve or Cain to the complete obedience of Y'shua to the confused and often dismayed Peter, our actions speak much louder than words ever could.

Maintaining a firm foundation in Genesis helps us retain Biblical Authority, it reminds us that our first response to the ideas of man is: does this new idea meet the biblical standard? Is that new idea compatible and consistent with the lessons we learn in the Bible? When others try to convince us of something that conflicts with the Bible their passion may seem to obscure their view, be aware that their passion doesn't cloud your judgement as well. Generally, people are too easily convinced but the old saying if something sounds too good be true it probably is reminds us to be careful of these new ideas also. God will not compromise His words, His action are consistent and He insists that we do things His way. Abraham, being willing to offer Issac, Joseph's patience in prison are other lessons we learn in Genesis that display how God's promises to provide for the faithful are absolute. When we display that uncompromising and unwavering faith we have access to the same blessings that Abraham, Issac, Jacob, Joseph and all of those Bible characters enjoyed. Now that we once again have established a firm foundation in Genesis, let's examine a few places where some people see those contradictions. I an confident that God will remain consistent and we will find those problems don't come from God, they belong to us.

CHAPTER 2

ONE OF THE major problems with understanding the Bible is translating it away from the original language. Hebrew culture during the centuries in which the Bible was written is very different than our modern culture today. History reveals that the English language is nothing like it was when the Bible was first translated into English so just because we might be speaking English we may be defining words quite differently. Many years ago I had the opportunity to visit several countries in Europe. During that visit I noticed that the world does not revolve around my American culture. The tour guide was from London and even though he was speaking English there was definitely a communication problem. He was speaking What I could call English, English and I was speaking American English and even though we could understand the words, we were defining those words differently. One particular evening as a group walked from a museum it was dark, I mentioned a flashlight and he wondered why I wanted to take a picture. To me this was silly, I wanted to see where we were going and he wanted to start a fire because he offered a torch. In America a flashlight is that small hand held lantern with batteries but in London a flash light is used with a camera and a torch is not a fire on a stick but a lantern with batteries. Confusion reigns when we don't define words the same and it is no different in the Bible.

Another problem we encounter is what value we assign to the words we use, the word lesson, should have much more value than the word story but instead of teaching our children Bible lessons we simply read them Bible stories. What message does that send to our young people? Some parents send their children to private or Christian schools and then allow their children to see their parents not placing the same value on what those schools teach. Our actions reveal how much value we place on Biblical Authority, the people around us see it and our Creator sees it as well. Failing to assign real value to the words and lessons we find in our Bible degrades it to nothing more than another book, a fairy tale that is full of nice stories. The way we live our lives displays for everyone to see exactly what value we place on the words we find in our Bible. Biblical Authority must be maintained if we are to understand how we fit into creation and how our Creator designed us to live.

Let's begin in Genesis during creation week and find out why some people think there were people before Adam. In Genesis 1:26 God said let's make man, in the next verse we read that God created man and in Genesis 2:7 we see that God formed man. So how does the use of these 3 words confuse the timeline during creation week? Some want to read into the lesson while others are trying to justify millions of years of evolution before Adam. If we look closely at the words make and create could be used interchangeably, the problem is the word in chapter 2, formed. Before we look at any Hebrew, let's see if there is any clues in the English. Look at the surrounding verses in chapters 1 and 2, basically chapter 1 reveals what God created from God's point of view. Chapter 2 tells us how God did what He did from Adam's point of view. They are almost inverted mirror images. Chapter 1 ends on the seventh day while chapter 2 begins on day 7.

Consider this; if we were to describe how to make a bird house, we could also say build a birdhouse or we could say create a beautiful birdhouse. All of these choices are acceptable and there is no real controversy in the phrase. When we begin to describe the way the birdhouse is made we could say that we cut the boards or that the boards are sawn to length. Again either way works Cut lets us know what was done while the word sawn tells us how it was done. Yes, people who study scripture do get involved in these questions, what we need to keep in mind is the consistency of the Bible. So we can see that even in English if we maintain Biblical Authority, we find the Bible is consistent. Paul write in Romans 5 that death reigned from Adam to Moses. If we consider there was no death before Adam sinned we would be correct, however we need to remember that Adam's sin brought death into the world. No death prior to Adam would mean that an entire group of people lived sin free until the serpent spoke to Eve and that is not consistent with what the Bible reveals. In 1 Corinthians 15 Paul compares Adam to Y'shua, Why would Paul make this comparison if Adam was not the first? He wouldn't, Paul studied the Torah and the prophets and had an understanding that only a devoted scholar achieves. Together with his visit from Y'shua on the road Paul knew very well how to compare Adam to Y'shua. For those who are familiar with Deuteronomy 17:16 which tells us we need 2 or more witnesses for something to be true, lets look at the Hebrew.

In Genesis 1:26 we see the Hebrew word עשה (pronounced "ah-sah") used in the form הנעשׂה (na -a -sey) now if you don't read Hebrew don't worry and if you want to verify this (and I hope you do) check any good concordance or lexicon. The Hebrew pronounced *Na - a - sey* means the three words in English let us make. in the next verse there is a different Hebrew word for "and created" which is closely related to the Hebrew word used in chapter 2:7 "formed." Are you beginning to see how translation and definition can alter our understanding? But that doesn't mean it should alter our faith or our Biblical Authority. Translators will use words which agree with their world view, if someone has a desire to sway our opinion they use words which lead us in the direction of their way of thinking. So if we read a translation which was edited by someone who accepts the earth is older than the Bible tells us it is then we must be extra careful to examine the words and make sure we hold onto the consistent Biblical standard.

Many of the same people who would claim that Adam was formed after a created "cave man" of a long past era try to justify their faith. "Those are good stories" they say, almost tongue in cheek. By their own admission they don't believe the Bible's account of creation but they try to grasp the concept of Revelation. Somehow in their mind, scripture has been twisted and perverted to sustain a belief that God needed millions of years to form the earth and have it just right when Adam and Eve were formed. During the time of Martin Luther, in the 16th century, just the opposite was taking place. The people of that time had formed a belief that God could have simply spoken and completed His work in less than one day. Luther's response was to hold fast to the Biblical Authority and that should be our response as well. To paraphrase Luther; God is much smarter than we are and we should consider there is a reason for Him doing things the way He did. Certainly God didn't need 6 days of work and a day of rest, He does this to establish our work week. Because He is our prime example and after all it is His universe and we must play be His rules.

That was an easy contradiction to satisfy using language, culture and history to examine if Adam was indeed the first human according to the Bible. Lets stay in Genesis for our next adventure, the cradle of civilization. Because of the familiar names of rivers and land used in Genesis chapter 2, we tend to get confused and begin thinking that these are the same rivers and land masses before and after the flood of Noah. There is no scriptural support for this and in fact Genesis 6:13 God tells Noah that He will destroy man along with the earth. Did you get that? God said He would destroy the earth along with man, that should be sufficient proof that the land mass where the Garden of Eden once existed was destroyed about 4,000 years ago but I know we need at least one more witness. Genesis 9:11 God tells Noah never again will a flood destroy the earth and 2 Peter 3:6–7 Peter write about the flood destroying the world. There are more witnesses in the Bible but I think you get the idea. The earth which was in the beginning a single land mass surrounded by water; Genesis 1:9 all the waters were gathered together in one place. If all of the water is in one place there are no land masses separating them. When God created this earth there was one body of water and one land mass. During Noah's flood as the land mass was completely destroyed, this same cataclysmic event allowed new land masses to form and as the water receded the earth as we know it came into existence.

This is a good place to interject what I like to call a Biblical timeline fundamental. Some Bible teachers suggest that there was technology before the flood that could explain how the pyramids were built. According to the Bible it would be impossible for the pyramids to exist before the flood. There are today scientists trying to replicate the way large hewn stones were moved by these primitive people. According to the Bible, the earth was completely destroyed approximately 4, 000 years ago, so the pyramids and everything else really are not that old. Consider this; Noah's son Shem being a righteous man would have had access to the technology that could have been used to build the pyramids. During the time that Shem lived after the flood would have been plenty of time to accomplish not only the Pyramids but many other miraculous construction projects which we attribute the the ancients. Then when Shem died shortly after Abraham, those projects suddenly stopped and the technology that was available died with Shem. Most people don't know that Shem lived about 23 years after Abraham died. I will freely admit there is not enough evidence in the Bible to prove that Shem was responsible for any large construction projects all I am suggesting is the possibility that the knowledge Shem had could have been used until his death.

There is a theory that the farther from creation we are the less knowledge we have. That is a friendly way to say the farther we are from create the dumber we are and we can take that both spiritually and physically. When we don't believe the creation lesson as it is in the Bible we don't have all of the information we need to make a wise judgement. Placing our faith in man instead of our Creator has consistently proven to be a bad choice. History teaches us that every time men turn away from the Bible, God allows their own selfishness to destroy them. We see that before the flood when even God was sorry he created man and again at Mount Sinai with the golden calf and again just before the Babylonian exile. More recently we see how Hitler was able to persuade many people to join him and the consequences of that were horrific because they were following man and not God. Failure to maintain Biblical Authority continues to plague humanity, in the United States today we see the result of removing not only prayer from our schools but removing God as well. Increased drug use, increased violence and increased sexually transmitted diseases are just a few of the repercussions we deal with as a result of compromising our Biblical Authority.

Back to the contradictions, there is a question concerning the amount of time the Hebrew people were actually in Egypt. Some say 400 years while other say something different. What does the Bible tell us about it? Let's look at what information is in the Bible about this. Genesis 12:2 God tells Abraham "I will make you a great nation" so the nation of Israel actually begins with Abraham. The Egyptian affliction of the Hebrew (Genesis 15) didn't begin after the sons of Jacob were there but years before in Genesis 21. Hagar was Egyptian and by Biblical following of genealogy so was Ishmael, so in Gen. 21:9 when Ishmael mocks Issac that is when the affliction of Israel begins. This is 30 years after the promise God made to Abraham which is how Moses is able to write in Exodus 12:41 that finally after 430 years the the children of Abraham would be free from the mocking of the Egyptians. The Hebrew people were physically only in Egypt for 215 Years when you follow the timeline.

Are you beginning to see how reading what is actually written on the pages is consistent while trying to force our tradition and mixed up ideas onto those pages adds inconsistency and contradiction? When we keep the Biblical

Authority and we read something that we don't understand we remind ourselves that *we* are confused. When we fail to keep Biblical Authority we think the Bible is confused. All of the confusion, inconsistencies and the contradictions belong to people not God, His word is Perfect and consistent.

When I began actually studying the Bible, I quickly realized that many of the things I had been taught were not accurate. Like most modern western Christians I was taught as a child growing up in the 1970's to think that Christians were more special than anyone else. Then came the phrase that God loves everyone, which is true and makes sense but wasn't consistent with the previous we are better than you mentality. The church my family attended regularly didn't have the same doctrine that the church just down the street had even though both claimed to be Christian churches. I wondered how people who claimed to be Christian could be so different when they were reading from the same Bible. When I was abut 6 or 7 years old my piano teacher was the wife of the pastor down the street. She would explain that the only real difference was in the way different churches worshipped. "Some people like a more refined service with lots of preaching and other people like more music and that's why you need to practice piano" she said. Now I can look back and realize these are simply more man made inconsistencies.

When Adam and Even defied God, sin and death brought confusion and evil into the world. since that time men and women have been trying to walk that fine line of what can I get away with and still be okay with God. People in general stopped doing their best to please their Creator and began pleasing themselves thinking there was no way for us to be happy and God to be happy at the same time. Eve's conversation with the serpent reveals our failure to faithfully believe the word of God. Eve couldn't resist adding to what she and Adam were told. She added we shouldn't even touch it but that was never part of God's word. The only instruction was not to eat it. The Bible is consistent and when we adhere to it we receive the blessing that God wants to give us but when we choose to defy God we open the door to confusion and are unable to recognize the blessing God wants us to have. Think of it this way, when we try to put together something with a lot of pieces we can either use the instructions or we can try to figure it out on our own. Sooner or later we either look at the picture to see what we are building should look like or we give up and read the instructions. Having put together everything from children toys to houses, it is much easier to follow the instructions when they are consistent and clear. When the instructions are jumbled and confusing then we need to look at the picture to find what it should look like.

Studying the Bible is much different than reading a novel. When I was in school, the teacher would have us read a book and either quiz us on the content or have us give the dreaded "book report." Both quiz and report would include what happened in the book and who the characters were, but that really didn't train us for real study. Bible study requires time and notes. Time to really read what is on the pages and to compare one passage with another that is often chapters or books apart. Notes to keep track of all the things we need to look at further. I keep a 3 ring binder for notes now because the margins in my Bibles were not large enough for all of my notes and since I use more than 1 translation I had no way to keep tack other than to put everything in one place. There are also some notes in there from outside sources like Josephus for history and rabbinic writing for culture reference and a few Apocrypha sources as well. While These outside resources are important for reference they don't hold the same importance as the the Bible.

Defusing the confusion about what the Bible really tells us can be challenging but not impossible. Proper study begins with prayer and a desire to learn, studying because we think it is a chore or something we should just do is an attitude that can distract us from our goal which should be to know God on a more intimate level than we did when we began. Deuteronomy 29 tells us there are some things God will keep secret from us but what He has given us is ours and our children's. We should understand from this that the Bible, what God has already told us, has no secrets in it because God has already given it to us. Contained on the pages of our Bibles are all the lessons we need to live our lives the way that God created us to live. When we add tradition and differing church doctrine to Scripture we have a recipe for confusion and inconsistencies which Satan will use to separate us from God if we let him.

Now that we've had a chance to satisfy some easy contradictions and get a feel for how to avoid them, let's get started with some that are not so easy and maybe less than comfortable. Really reading what is in the Bible will challenge what you have been trained to think and the way you view the world. Using the Bible as the standard you use to compare new ideas, old ideas, church doctrine and even traditions can be as scary as it is rewarding but it is worthwhile. when you use Biblical Authority others will question and ridicule, even good church going Christians will think you have joined some kind of cult or gone over the edge because you are showing your faith at work in your life. I had one preacher tell me during a face to face conversation,"Well you can't believe everything that's in the Bible." I can and I do, if that preacher can't maybe that person needs to find another source of employment because they don't need to be leading a church. Plain and simply, we either choose to believe the Bible or we don't, we don't have the luxury to pick and choose what scripture is important and what isn't. While each of us as individuals are given certain skills which God uses to build His kingdom, all of these are equally important. Not every person is called to deliver the same message, some teach grace, some teach obedience and some teach repentance and some teach other things and all of these are equally necessary to build the Kingdom of God.

CHAPTER 3

During a conversation with a pastor, I asked what he thought of a project that I am involved with. This project challenges people to improve their life by making small changes to their daily routine. The changes they make actually come from the bible and each one is something that God asks us to do. He told me it was a good idea and in his words, "but there is no scripture in it." That seemed odd to me because the whole thing is Bible based and each change is backed by a Bible passage. After I thought about his response I came to the realization that he didn't believe the Bible. Paul's second letter to Timothy reads in part; that all scripture is inspirational of God and profitable. When Paul wrote this there was no New Testament, all Paul knew to reference as scripture was the Torah, the Prophets and the other writing that make up our Old Testament or in Hebrew the Tanakh. I chose not to include any New Testament passages in my project because I did't want people to confuse Salvation with following God's instructions, one person was accusing me of not including his concept of scripture in that project. Don't allow me to confuse you about this, when Paul writes that ***all*** scripture is valuable I believe he meant all. Paul may or may not have known about the letters that would become known to us as the Gospels, he was writing about what he knew and understood.

I had to remember the passage from Colossians 2, let no man judge you, which we can remove the confusion about right now. Some read this verse and think that is goes along with the Matthew 7 verse judge not, but these are 2 completely separate lessons. In Matthew Y'shua is teaching only his disciples, they were the only ones there on the hillside with him. What he is saying in this verse is if you judge someone you will be held to the same standard. Certainly we can hold each other accountable for our actions without being judgmental. Defining the words the way they were translated and the way we use them today might help here. According to Webster's 1828 definition, judge from the Matthew 7 verse is defined as to pass a severe sentence. The difference is not that you are holding someone accountable by comparing their actions, you have already awarded punishment in this situation. the confusion is that we don't understand the definition of the translation. In other words, don't judge means not to punish in this verse, it doesn't mean not to compare actions with Biblical Authority.

On to the Colossians verse, Don't let any man Judge you, Paul in the previous verses lays a foundation of careful study. He warns against allowing someone to undermine Biblical Authority in verse 8 basically writing don't be fooled by some fast talking preacher who is telling you exactly what you *want* to hear or be taken in by fancy decorations or empty lies. He is preparing you for the next lesson that some people will fall for these things and they will try to convince you that because you are holding on to Biblical Authority you are wrong. The same thing that was happening with the Colossians the is happening among churches today. The traditions and the doctrines of our modern churches reflects more than just a different way to worship, they have become a different way to believe. Some denominations believe you can't get to Heaven unless you are a member of their church, where's that in the Bible? Paul is warning us that there are some who will accuse you of doing something wrong when you haven't done anything right or wrong yet. Another lesson we learn from this part of Colossians is Solomon was right when he wrote "there is nothing new under the sun." Today we see infighting among denominations when we should be unified as the body to build the kingdom but because we don't do it my way or your way we choose not to get along. Here is a wild idea, let's do it God's way, after all He is the one who wrote the rule book right? His Universe, His rules.

There are 2 more contradictions resolved and I know I won't be able to get to all of them but if you follow the example of Biblical Authority and study by the time you're finished with this book, you should have the tools you need to resolve your favorite contradiction from the Bible. Here is a handy hint; while you are studying, stop and think if there is a lesson from another part of the Bible that is familiar to what you are reading. If there is a famil-iar word or idea go to it and include it in your reading, make a note that those verses could go together in some way. Peter writes that Paul is hard to understand because he is constantly quoting from the what we know as the Old Testament (and sometimes from other places) but he is writing it in a way that the people he is writing to should be able to comprehend. For instance some translations of Romans has Paul using circumcision as an outward sign, of course this is ridiculous. Only men could be circumcised, how would a woman be able to show she is keeping a covenant with God? by following His instructions just like the men should have been doing.

This leads me to a big controversy, were women really treated as second class citizens in the Bible? let's see what the Bible has to say about it. We learn in Genesis that Adam wad made first from the earth. I know there is a joke about Adam and all men being bags of dirt but that's okay, we'll let that one go. Eve, on the other hand was made from one of Adams ribs. Let's consider why God who could have simply made Eve from dirt as well made Eve from a rib of Adam after he had breathed the breath of life into Adam. God didn't want Eve to ever be considered a bag of dirt, in fact because of the order of creation women hold a much higher place in society than we expect. Here is a timeline to help;

1. God makes Adam
2. God givesAdam a soul and the breath of life which is the ability to communicate thoughts and ideas.
3. God puts Adam to sleep and uses a rib to make Eve.

What can we learn from this? Ladies sit back and enjoy, men; you might not like what you learn here. The general concept is because Adam was made first men are more important than women, there is no Biblical support for that anywhere in the Bible. Man was made from the earth, part of creation, then God gave man a soul and the ability to communicate on a more complex level than the animals. Even animals have a soul but lack that breath of God so we are on a higher level than they. Eve being made from a rib after that breath of life is place into Adam is now on a completely different level of understanding which is another reason women think differently than men do.

Now think about why God used a rib, He could have used a toe or a arm but there is something special about a rib. Ribs are the cage of protection around the vital organs in our chest. If you have ever cracked or broken a rib then you know exactly what I mean. an injured rib is a pain unlike any other, it hurts to breath. Coughing and laughing can be unbearable and a sneeze; the world ends. God uses a rib to form Eve because this gives her control over the man's most vital organ; the heart. God gave Woman complete control over a man's happiness, sadness and life. What man who understands this would ever think a woman is beneath him or is second class? different absolutely, second to him; never. There are several places in the Bible that support this concept, one of those is in Exodus. When Moses was up on the mountain getting instructions, the people thought he had been there too long. They ask Aaron to make a god for them and to he first tried to avoid the problem. When the men said we don't know what happened to Mose make us a god Aaron had an idea, he told them to bring the earrings of their wives and children hoping their wives would say no! Unfortunately, Aaron received the gold and made a calf, then lied to Moses about it saying I threw the gold in the fire an a calf came out. The point I'm making is that Aaron tried to defuse the problem by depending on the women, When they went along with their husbands and gave the gold Aaron didn't have a choice but he was certainly hoping that the women wouldn't give up their gold for a statue.

Another place we see women boldly confronting evil is Judges 4 with Deborah who was a prophetess and a judge. Her husband is named and we know that is important because he must have been a Godly man. We understand this because of what Paul writes in 1 corinthians about a covering (spiritual, not physical). here is where it gets a little tricky to explain and I will try to make this as easy as possible. Because Adam was first to receive the breath of life, a woman needs the spiritual covering of a man to give her spiritual guidance not because she isn't completely capable but because God passed the breath of life to Eve through Adam's rib. This can come from a father, a husband, a son or a spiritual leader of a fellowship. Again, not because the woman is unable on her own but because God designed us this way and a Godly man should lead in every aspect of life. This concept here downplays the idea that there are assigned jobs for men and women. Sorry guys but you are chosen by God to lead in everything we do. In today's society men should be the first to change diapers, do the dishes, vacuum the floor; you get the idea. Men are to lead and not designate. women are there to help, just as Eve was there to be a "helpmeet" for Adam. That is a word no longer used in English but it mean to come together to help. Eve was to help tend the garden, Adam may have been shown what to do first but Eve was to be right there by his side. Did that end when they went home at dark? no, Adam would have been right there gathering whatever was for supper making sure Eve wasn't including the fruit from the tree of the Knowledge of good and evil.… OOPS! Yes because Adam ate as well both men, women and all of creation suffer (which could lead into a whole other topic.)

Are you beginning to get a different picture than you were taught? lets look at a Shunammite woman from 2 kings chapter 4 and following. Elisha comes to the area and she convinced her husband to build a room for the prophet to stay in while he was near. Elisha was grateful and gave the woman a son. As the son grew something happened one day and he died, the woman who is never named went to the field and asked for a donkey and a servant to go to the prophet. When her husband questioned this her response was one word; "shalom." Her answer meant I don't have time for your chaos right now, I have something important to do. When she arrived at the prophet's house the servant began to ask her questions and she quite abruptly cut him off with the same response; "Shalom." I don't have time for your manly chaos now this is important. In this example we see a woman rebuking not only her husband (in private) but a servant as well (again not in front of anyone.) Her manner speaks volumes to how women were to be properly treated in the Bible. By the way Elisha brought the boy back from the place of the dead and there is a possibility that child is none other than Jonah although he is not named in this lesson.

Women are Absolutely not second class citizens in the Bible, they understood they were different than men but that difference is what made them better. Because they had control over man's heart they understood the importance of their position, because women understood their extremely important position they were comfortable being "above the fray" as the saying is. Today Women try to be equal, I will agree that our culture makes it necessary for women to receive equal pay for equal work, no question about that but I will question if men or women are better today than they were when God first created them, and I don't think they are. I could argue that humanity as a whole is much worse than God intended for us to be and I believe we can attribute that to our failure to uphold Biblical Authority.

Have you ever wondered why God would give a young innocent Mary the choice of mothering His unique son?

Our Creator himself asks Mary through the angel if she is willing to mother the one He would anoint. If women were second class citizens would God ask Mary's permission? If women were lower than men in any way would Y'shua have bothered to waist any time with them? (think of the women at the well and the adulterous woman that we will get to later.) So why do we think that women in the Bible were less than what they really were? because we were taught to think that way. Satan loves to use our modern culture to confuse and twist scripture. He tries to convince us that the world will drastically implode if everyone would follow God's instructions. He tries to tell us that we are now enlightened and empowered and know more than God does. That sounds exactly like what he told Eve in the garden. "If you eat it you will be just like God" no they were not just like God, they brought sin and death into the world where God brings life. In the battle of the sexes, where man once revered women and were their spiritual covering, women have chosen to go their own way and try as they would to be equal, some are dissatisfied and dismayed that they are still different. My wife is a much better "people person" than I am, she enjoys her job working in a hospital where she is able to heal wounds and comfort the oppressed. I am terrible at healing and much more comfortable inflicting wounds and irritating people because of my past and this ministry thing is strange to me but God chooses us we don't choose Him as John writes in chapter 15. Men, if you still think women are the weaker sex or second class citizens, ask yourself this question; where would we be today without Eve, Rebecca, Deborah, Rehab, ruth, Mary and a long list of other names that may or may not be mentioned in the Bible. Each one of these women held the life of a man in the palm of their hand at some point including the life of Y'shua. allow that to "think in" for a moment.

This may be a good place to address one of the most misunderstood teachings that Y'shua ever spoke about and that is divorce. Many good pastors have taught that the only reason for divorce is adultery and they would almost be correct if it were not for a little thing called consistency. John writes that Y'shua is the word and became flesh, or the physical manifestation of everything that God spoke and that includes His instructions. If that is true as Christians proclaim, then there is no way that Y'shua could have taught that the only reason for divorce is adultery because that would mean he would be contradicting himself as the word of God which is true and perfect. So where's the problem? begin with what God told Moses about divorce. In Deuteronomy 24 we read in English when a man no longer finds favor, or is displeased or no longer finds pleasure he can write a bill of divorce. This is not as simple as we have been led to believe. The word translated as favor or pleasing is the Hebrew word for grace (yes there is grace in the Old Testament) so there must be a really good reason that there would no longer be grace in the home. Although it was the man's responsibility to sit down a write out a long and very detailed explanation of why the divorce needed to happen, the woman was completely within her duty to remove grace from the home if she needed to. To put it another way if the woman was being mistreated, or the husband was not being a good provider and spiritual covering the wife had a duty to remove grace from the home and receive a divorce. Of course adultery was a reason as well but not the only reason according to the word of God which Y'shua could not violate.

What about marrying a virgin or a divorced woman? those ruling were only for the Levite priests. When we study about the law, we need to understand who the instructions are for. There are instructions that are for everyone and there are instructions for specific people. Some are only for men and some for women while some are for only children and others for animals. When we understand who the instruction applies to then we know how to apply it to our live today if and when we need to. There were times when a brother was to take his deceased brother's wife as his own to make sure the family unit continued, isn't that marrying someone who is not a virgin? of course it is. There are some things we need to realize that only make sense in the minds of people who want to see controversy and inconsistencies.

So how does the teaching of Y'shua in Matthew 5 not contradict what is being taught in Deuteronomy? The translation is part of the problem here because the Greek word used was also translated as idolatry, but that is only part of the problem. Y'shua was very specific when he spoke, the phrase "you have heard it said" he uses almost exclusively to address the rules the Pharisee's put into place to add to or subtract from the law of Moses which is the word of God. Y'shua uses the phrase "it is written" to refer to the law it's self. When he is teaching his disciples in Matt. 5 he begins you have heard, meaning he is speaking about thePharisees who were violating the law by divorcing and remarrying divorced women which is clearly stated in Leviticus as a huge "no-no" for them. What he is stating here is that the only divorce option for a *priest* is because of adultery and by doing so Y'shua is again upholding Biblical Authority.

CHAPTER 4

Are you still here? not mad yet? Have I provoked some emotion that either you want to say NO!! there's no way or is that really in the Bible? One of the most familiar Psalms is Psalm 23. I decided that for one week I would ask people about it, anyone I came into contact with from checkout people in the grocery store to workers at Walmart, if they began a conversation I would find a way to bring it to Psalm 23. What I wanted to know is simply this, have you ever hear of it? that's all I wanted to know. The majority of people in my local mid Atlantic area had heard of psalm 23, they may not have known it as a psalm but they remembered either the Lord is my shepherd or yea though I walk through the valley of the shadow of death. I even know Joe Biden, Vise President under Barak Obama heard Psalm 23 one time for sure. When he was a Senator from Delaware he attended a dinner which I attended as well and Psalm 23 was recited at that dinner. Psalm 23 is read at practically every funeral there is in the modern Christian church. Sunday school classes memorize it and is s familiar as the lord's prayer. The question is why? What makes Psalm 23 so familiar to people? is it a Psalm of comfort or hope? What was David trying to tell us as he wrote Psalm 23?

David knew the job of a shepherd was to care for the animals he was responsible for. David equated that responsibility to God taking care of us as individuals when he wrote; God is My shepherd. Because God is my shepherd I will not do without anything I need to live a good life. Verse 2 isn't about wanting meaningless stuff, it is about having exactly what we need when we need it, food, shelter water and comfort. Because God wants me to have those things He will make sure I have them. Have you ever wondered about the orphans and homeless before it was popular to wonder about the orphans and the homeless? Even before the stories about Oliver Twist and tiny Tim. during the earliest part of the first millennium after the resurrection. How were the orphans and the homeless treated? Mostly it depended on which country you were in, if you lived in a warmer climate you did fairly well eating whatever grew wild all year long. If you lived in a colder climate you may not be so fortunate, but God has a way of caring for His creation. Even in the worst and most disgusting part of history the orphans and homeless were cared for, in a way. if you could work you were expected t work for your food, when you could not work there was debtor's prison; a place you would eat and be warm in the cold weather but could never be freed from. As society progressed into our current civilization, the decision was made to care for the widows and orphans but in a way that lacks any real compassion. These earliest forms of welfare lacked any way for those who received it to recover. Today all over the world, many of these same models remain, there is help but the ones receiving help have no way to come back as active members of society. In the United States welfare has become a way of life and unfortunately in other countries it is either prison or debtors colonies or slave labor that drives the system. God on the other hand, had a different idea, He would give us exactly what we needed not just to survive but to succeed. God would not let us do without what we need to benefit others and ourself. Our Creator designed us with a gift that when we use it to benefit someone else, it benefits us as well.

Psalm 23 is a psalm of submission, we submit to God's will because he leads us to where we can benefit, He leads us to the calm places where we are not continually tested and harassed. God restores us as well, making sure that we are healthy, satisfied and prepared for whatever might come our way. Our Creator offers us the luxury of being blessed with everything He chooses to give us, submitting to His will allows us to recognize those blessings for what they are. Imagine being able to lie down in a lush green pasture beside a calm, still, crystal clear lake, that was the ultimate vacation during David's life. Being rejuvenated, refreshed and made completely whole simply because that is what our God wants for us is a possibility today and not just a daydream.

The most familiar verse in the Psalm is Yea though I walk through the valley of the shadow of death, let's stop right there and examine this odd phrase. First let's ask who casts a shadow of death? when God is the light for us to be walking in shadow there must be something between God and us. So who is it that tries to come between man and our Creator? who else but Satan. What David is explaining with this is even when Satan tries to drive a wedge between God and us, God is still right here. I know that sometimes it doesn't feel like it but He is always here and available and David is reenforcing that very idea. He know that God will be there and he can feel him because of the next verse, your rod and staff comfort me. Isn't a rod and staff the same thing? Not here they aren't, When this was translated into English rod was used interchangeably with discipline and support. Bread is the staff of life, how deep I could wind this literally and metaphorically would take another book, but I will simply interject Ezekiel 4:16 in part "he said to me, Son of man, behold, I will break the staff of bread in Jerusalem." So David reveals here that Gods discipline (His instructions) and His bread (Y'shua) comforts. Are you totally blown away by David's prophetic writing? wait until we get to the end of this Psalm!

If God prepares a table for us in the presence of our enemy, what doe it look like in our mind today? Some may answer Thanksgiving dinner for some families, but how would David view this concept. Remember Middle Eastern culture during David's reign was much different than our Western culture today, People would eat in a reclining position, sitting upright was reserved for negotiation. Body language was important and even though we consider the ancients as cavemen, savages or uncivilized, many of their customs survived to our civilization today. So what does a table in front of my enemy look like? Consider a negotiation, more specifically when we are on God's side, the enemy trying to negotiate something more for himself than unconditional surrender. That's right, when we are on God's side we win and the enemy will surrender unconditionally, but don't get too comfortable yet, remember we need to be on God's side not just having God on our side, there is a difference.

David knew what it meant to be anointed with oil, Samuel anointed him years before. To be anointed you must first be chosen, and second you must submit to being anointed. If you have ever spilled cooking oil or olive oil, it can be difficult to clean up. For someone to allow another to pour this stuff all over your head you need to be in a submissive position. When we submit to God's will and authority we open ourselves to receive His blessings. God is not unlike a wealthy parent or other relative who is telling us that when we do things His way we get rewarded, when receiving blessing from God His rewards are better than we could ever imagine.

Finally David brings this lesson into perspective, if we do the things God wants us to do, good things and His mercy will be with us constantly. We will continue to receive His blessings, we will be forgiven when we mess things up or don't understand something as long as we are actively trying to please Him. when we give up and believe there is no way we could ever hope to be good enough that is exactly when we are not good enough. Not because of who we are but because we stopped trying, we gave up we allowed ourselves to be deceived because we didn't hold onto that Biblical Authority. The great thing about God is we don't have to get it perfect, but we need to do our best. If we do the best we can with the information we have David make the last proclamation in this Psalm; I will dwell in the hose of the LORD forever! Did David have the same vision that John had in Revelation 21? the new Jerusalem being lowered to earth. We don't know, there isn't enough information here but the language is certainly consistent throughout the Bible about it. Yes, David was certainly a prophet and the key to understanding the things he wrote is to view them as prophecy. Not as a fortune teller tries to show the future but as a real prophet, someone who proclaims we need to follow God's instructions because that was the primary job of real prophet.

When we use the word prophet it conjures a picture i our minds of some old person who is locked in room writing down the things he hears directly from God. We need to change that view of a prophet, The few prophets we have in the Bible were ordinary people, living ordinary lives. Read the opening verse of Amos, he was a herdsman, Jeremiah was the son of a priest and should have been trained to continue that job. Ezekiel was a priest, Zachariah was the Grandson of the prophet Iddo, but none of the famous prophets actually wanted that job. The picture which we have in our mind of an old man writing down countless premonitions is more of a Nostradamus tale and not a Bible lesson. When God gave a vision to someone, he or she would go to the Temple and speak to the priests, the scribe would write down everything that was said and keep the record of the record until it either proved true or false. In the opening verse of Amos we see that it was written after Amos had predicted an earthquake 2 years prior. That was the proof the priests needed to know that he had actually heard from God. Can you imagine if we had to wait 2 years today for any real proof of something?

The primary message from any of the prophets was to obey God, it is that easy. Of course they would also tell of the consequences for their disobedience as well and if it happened then everyone knew that prophet was really hearing from Heaven. Being a prophet wasn't an easy chore, along with the ridicule there was the chance that someone (usually the King) wouldn't like what you were told by God to speak. That meant there was a really good chance the king would have you killed. Earthly kings get very sensitive about people telling them they are wrong. Hebrews 11:37 recounts of the tragic end of certain prophets "They were stoned, they were sawn asunder, were tempted, were slain with the sword: destitute." Being a prophet definitely had it's challenges and was not something to be sought after.

So are there any contradictions in the prophets? Not if you rely on Biblical Authority, but we can test a few and see what happens. Let's begin in Jeremiah, 2 times in Jeremiah God reminds us of a promise He made in Exodus 19:5 If we obey the voice (word) of God we will be special to him. In Jeremiah Chapters 7 and 11 God tells us if we obey His voice we will be His people and He will be our God. Twice more God speaks and tells us that He will put His words in our hearts and He will be our God. There is a continuous concept from Exodus even through Isaiah chapter 56 which is all about if we obey God, He will not separate us from Himself, then through Jeremiah and the rest of the Psalms and other prophets.

Naturally this concept continues throughout the New Testament as well, when Y'shua stops in the middle of teaching the disciples how to receive what they are asking for in prayer and gives this warning," If you love me, Keep my commands." The Gospel accounts of everything Y'shua said and did reflect that he is teaching to obey the word of the Father above all else, constantly irritating the Pharisees and the rules they added to the word of God. Paul agrees when he writes in Romans 3, that faith establishes the law which is the word of God. Then on to John who gives us the Biblical definition of sin in 1 John 3:4 Sin is the violation of the law.

Understand that the the instructions we received at Mount Sinai do not offer salvation, that is a completely different topic, (and I will get to that later) the point I am trying to make here is that the prophets and the Gospels are clear and consistent that we display our love and submission to our Creator by following His instructions, that is what makes us special to Him and what makes us His. Just because God loves the whole world doesn't mean He condones the actions of the world. What makes us special to Him is our actions more than our words. We can say we love our God but if we continue to do the things God hates our actions prove that we love the world more. We can say we love but if we continue to worship idols, steal, commit adultery and any other violation of the 10 commandments then where is the proof of love? Nowhere in any of the prophets (or any other part of the Bible) are we able to read that it is perfectly acceptable not to follow God's instructions.

Look at Isaiah 56, God tells us that even if the Eunuchs will guard the Sabbath, do what is right and keep follow His instructions they will have a place in His house and have a name which is better than having sons and daughters. This reenforces Exodus 12:49 there is 1law for the Hebrew (the term Jew had not been used yet in Exodus) and those who join themselves together with them maintaining Biblical Authority and continuity. Yet today there are people who will argue against the Bible because they believe there are separate rules for God's people and everyone else or those things were for those people in their time. I will challenge anyone to find in the Bible where God has not been consistent and if you keep the authority of the bible no one can find that because it isn't there.

Let's examine the difference between following God's instructions and receiving salvation. Being "born again" or "saved" are the modern Christian terms used to describe a person has accepted the sacrifice of Y'shua on a Roman cross and the resurrection which occurred afterward. Our Creator has accepted the blood of His perfect lamb as an atonement for our sin; the problem is that most people don't know what sin is or why it needed to be atoned for in the first place. Too often denominational doctrine fails to properly explain what sin is and try to define sin as anything that separates us from God. That separation is a result of sin and not the sin itself. Thankfully we have John's first letter to give us a Biblical definition of sin—1 John 3:4 sin is a violation of the law. Because we know that the word law in this passage relates directly to the first five books of the Bible we are able to define sin as failing to follow the instructions given to us through Moses at Mount Sinai.

Here is where we usually find someone screaming we are not under the law we are under grace! Sometimes they will claim legalism or that's been done away with, and we will get to that very shortly but let's take one step at a time. According to John sin is failing to follow God's instructions that we received in the desert so any atonement for that failure must be connected directly to Mount Sinai. What happened at Mount Sinai that would cause God to inflict the death penalty on the very people He brought out of slavery in Egypt? Allow me to lay this out as best I am able in this format.

The Hebrews are in Egypt; we learn in Exodus that Mose was sent back to Egypt to lead the children of Abraham to the promised land. God didn't send Moses with a list of instructions and tell them they had to get it right before they could leave so there can be no violation of the law yet.

Pharaoh denies God who begins a series of plagues against Egypt which directly rebukes each of Egypts many gods including the last plague; death of the first born, destroying man who has called himself a god. Each of these plagues were against Egypt and not the Hebrew people so there is still no violation of the law.

The Hebrews are lead to Mount Sinai where God asks the question; in Exodus 19; to paraphrase—are you willing to do things My way? The people said yes not knowing yet what the instructions would be from this God of Abraham.

Our Creator personally visits the people in the desert and speaks to them from the top of the mountain and the people realize they were not ready. They beg Moses to be the intercessor and speak for God which he does. When the instructions were made known, Moses sacrifices oxen and uses half the blood to cover the alter and the other half he sprinkles on the people effectively sealing a blood covenant between God and the mixed multitude of people who were there that had just agreed to follow God's instructions. Now the people know and understand what the instructions are. but there is no mention of a failure to follow those instructions until exodus 32.

The people became impatient and refused to wait for Moses to return from the mountain top and caused Aaron to make a god for them out of gold. Wait! here is a violation of the first instruction God spoke to the people. You will put no other gods in my face, and here we have the people creating the golden calf. Here it is; the people had failed to follow the instructions and had broken the blood covenant between them and God.

Our Creator was furious and instructed Moses to wait while He was going to kill them all and begin again this time with Moses. The only reason that didn't happen was because Moses himself pleaded for the people and asked God to find another way. Our Creator in His ultimate wisdom designed a sacrificial system as a constant reminder to the people that they had broken the blood covenant and that death would be the price. The sacrifices were only a bookmark, a constant and continual reminder that our God demands payment for our violation. Every one understands that there was no way the blood of animals would ever be sufficient to repay for what we had done, the sacrifices were for us to remember that God would demand payment from us someday. So now we have a consistent connection from Mount Sinai to John's first letter, We know what sin is and we know what God demands as payment.

Because Y'shua was completely innocent, his blood was able to atone for our failures. That doesn't mean that because he paid the fine we can keep sinning though; Y'shua paid our debt and now we owe him. He is the one perfect example in the entire Bible of how we should live our lives and he asks us to be like him. He was constantly reminding people to "go and sin no more" and when the Pharisees challenged his authority to forgive sin he turns the question back on them which is consistent with Ezekiel 18:21–25 which basically reads that if a wicked person stops sinning and does what is right their sins will no longer be mentioned; but if a good person begins doing evil none of their good deeds will be mentioned. Y'shua remains consistent with the Biblical authority never adding to or taking anything away from the instructions given to us but why not John proclaims him to be the living word of the Father.

So why today are there so many Christian denominations proclaiming that the "law" is no longer valid? To turn the question back on them; Why would Y'shua who paid our debt for breaking the law throw it away? That would be like a judge paying your fine for you and then repealing the law after he had paid it. There is no consistency with that way of thinking and yet there are teachers and preachers who claim this insanity. There is so much misconception about why we should follow God's instructions that we too often miss the very point of them. First nowhere in the entire Bible will you read that keeping the law will ensure you a place in Heaven, it doesn't work that way. read the words in the Bible without the filter of religious thinking; Exodus 19:5 God's deal is this, if you do things My way you will be a special treasure to me. Nope no promise of Heaven here. Deuteronomy 5:33 Follow God's instructions so it will go well with you and you will have a long life. (my paraphrase) Ezekiel 11:20 hear my voice and follow my instructions and you will be my people and I will be your God. (Again, my paraphrase) These are just a few examples that the Bible is consistent with the message that following the instructions is the way we display our obedience to God the Father. The next time someone tries to convince you that we no longer need to follow God's instructions tell them they are right, we are free to ignore our Creator and be disobedient because following His instructions or keeping the law however you want to express it is not about salvation and it is not about getting into Heaven.

Following God's instruction's is about receiving and recognizing the blessings that God wants to give us.

When we are disobedient He will hold back the blessings just as any good parent will not reward bad behavior in a child. Our Creator chooses to reward obedience and blesses us abundantly and although sometimes it may seem as though good things happen to bad people; it is only in the short term if you want the long lasting kind of blessings God wants you to have live life the way He designed us to live and follow His instructions. Every one of the instructions we have fro God teach us how to love, they teach us how to love God and our neighbor. From the first commandment not to put any other gods in the face of our Creator to the most seemingly minute about using fair weights and measures, each one is a lesson on how to treat one another with respect and love.

These are only a few examples of how following God's instructions are not chained to salvation, to write a complete explanation and extrapolate all of the information would require volumes and would reveal the same answer. For those who still want more witnesses we can go to Ephesians 2:8 about salvation being a gift and it is a gift freely given but just as any gift it is useless unless you unwrap it and use it. Salvation also comes with a responsibility when we use it, if we receive a car as a gift that is only the beginning, a car requires taxes and tags, insurance and if you are going to drive it a license. Verse 9 reminds us that we can not earn our way into God's Kingdom, if we could we wouldn't need God. Verse 10 is our response to salvation and how we use it wisely. For we are His (God's) workmanship, now recreated in the image of Y'shua to do good works (follow the instructions) which God has previously established (at Mount Sinai) that we should walk in (do) them. Here even Paul makes the argument that there is a clear distinction between salvation and following the instructions, although one is connected to the other in one way they are separate as well.

John writes that Y'shua is the word made flesh, follow that back through the bible and we have the word is truth and light found in Palms and in Proverbs. We also see that in John 14:6 Y'shua is the way the truth and the light, all references to the instructions. Follow closely here; Y'shua also explains that a house divided can not stand (Mark 3:25) so with this information in one package how is it possible for the law to be abolished? it isn't possible and because the Bible reveals that Y'shua is indeed the law made flesh he can not abolish himself and he can not divide himself or he can not stand. So we have Y'shua the person and the instructions both separate but both very much the same. An example would be an apple, it is a fruit but it is also an apple at the same time both capable of occupying the same space at the same time because they are indeed one but separated by description at the same time.

In Genesis we read that the voice of God was walking, how is that possible? can a voice walk? Who was there with them in the garden? in Jeremiah we read that the word of God came to Jeremiah, this may be a little easier to think about with the same question, who came to Jeremiah? Because Y'shua is everything the Bible tells us he is then it is possible for us to consider and be consistent that he was there in the beginning, he is the word and he is the voice as well because John writes that nothing was made that he didn't make so when God spoke his voice as spirit went where the father sent him.

The controversies and the inconsistencies belong to us, we have distorted Scripture beyond recognition for the sake of reaching our destination as quickly and cheaply as possible. We have even removed personal responsibility proudly proclaiming we can simply think good thoughts and get into Heaven when thought the Bible our actions not our words or thoughts are what determines our future. Hopefully that will resolve the issue of works and salvation for most people, they are both important and even though they are separate they are designed to be used together. Now because that was the biggest controversy in the Bible the rest of should be easy, shouldn't it?

CHAPTER 5

Since we had so much fun with salvation and whether we should follow God's instructions let's look at what we should or shouldn't eat. Do you really understand what the Bible says about food? I'm not a nutritionalist and won't go into the argument about how healthy something is or isn't, instead I'll stick to scripture and allow Biblical authority to be the guide. First we need to establish what the bible considers food, this may seem easy but because we need to use the same definitions I'll begin in Genesis. The first time the concept of clean or unclean animals is written in the Bible is in Genesis 7:2 God tells Noah that he is to bring 7 pairs of clean animals but of the not clean animals only bring the male and the female. The question should be how did Noah know the difference? this was before Leviticus was written and even before we were told we could eat any meat at all so where does this come from? Actually verse 5 gives us the answer, Noah did *all* that God commanded him. Just because we don't have the complete transcript of the conversation we have enough to know that there was much more that God was telling Noah and I refuse to speculate on what might have been revealed to Noah but it would be safe to consider there was a great deal of information given about how he was to do everything to make certain the ark was ready for flood.

As we examine food we know that before the flood everyone was vegetarian, Something happens in chapter 9 and again we don't have the entire conversation recorded in the Bible but we have enough information to know that because the animals now owe their survival to man we are granted permission to use their offspring as a food source as a way of repaying their debt to us. There are certain restrictions included at this point about blood that are recorded and we can learn from what the people actually did post flood to know that certain animals were not considered edible. The post flood world was not the peaceful eden we might want to think it is, as the sons of Noah began to repopulate the earth they failed to follow God's instruction and instead remained in 1 place, the plains of Shinar. Then after the confusion of the languages they finally dispersed to dominate the world and it isn't until Genesis chapter 13 we see people keeping herds of animals once again, the first reference being that of Abel keeping a flock in Genesis 4. These herds or flocks were considered as being sheep, goats or cattle, camels, donkey's and oxen are typically mentioned separately as beasts of burden, not kept for food but for work.

Now the careful person would ask at this point why would Abel keep a flock if people were not using it for food, and that would be a very good question. IF we look at Genesis 4:4 we get the only clue but it isn't clear in English. The Bible reads that Abel brought the firstlings of his flock, the fat there of. This simply means that Able brought the absolute very best he could find among the animals under his care. Cain on the other hand brought a few fruits and vegetables, we should note here that this is often considered a sacrifice but the word translated in verse 4 as offering is not the same Hebrew word for sacrifice but considered more of a gift. So although many people have been taught to believe that Abel and Cain were making sacrifice as in killing the animals and burning them along with the fruit and vegetables that was probably not the intention of the offering. We should be able to reasonably conclude this was more like bringing a gift to Grandfather or bringing the best to be judged at a fair which is why when Cain's gift was second (or in this case last) place, he was angry. Of course he had only himself to blame, Abel brought the best he could find while Cain grabbed the first things he could. The point is, don't be fooled into thinking that because able had a flock to care for that they were being used for food because that permission wasn't given until after the flood.

Getting back to the flocks and the herds, no place do we read about people keeping odd beasts, we read about the certain animals (one translated as unicorn in Job 39) being so wild they could not be kept, so as post-flood mankind was establishing a new type of agriculture the language in the Bible properly reflects the practices. Sheep, goats and cattle were kept in flocks and easily guided from place to place as necessary but there is no mention of swine or other unclean animals being used for food from the flood through the book of Exodus. Not until Leviticus (technically beginning in 10:10) do we begin to get some instruction as what designates an animal clean or unclean. We could speculate that some cultures either from ignorance or necessity began to eat whatever they wanted but that is only speculation. While we don't have enough information to know exactly why God chooses to instruct us to avoid certain animals, we do know there are animals that match certain criteria which were not considered food.

The quick reference for which animals are food is this; if it has a split hoof and chews it's cud it's food. If it doesn't eat other dead animals or really disgusting stuff it's food. If it is in the water and has scales it's food. I'll admit I'm not a fan of eating bugs but grasshoppers, crickets and a few other bugs like them, are food and I have been told they are quite tasty. The things we are told to avoid are basically any animal that eats any other dead animal and that includes pigs, bears, dogs, cats, rats, bats, egles, vultures, shrimp, crabs and lobster. Now that we have a definition of what food is we can examine if anything has changed in the Bible to which would allow us to eat the things God told us to avoid.

Hebrew history from Mount Sinai until the end of the second Temple period was filled with turmoil. There were battles that were won and lost, famine, and as the Bible records; times the people would listen to God and times they didn't but through it all they tried to find a way to follow God's instructions sometimes too well. The Torah, the first five books of the Bible contain the instructions and twice we are reminded not to add anything or remove anything from those instructions. With the concept in mind the Torah has been considered a fence to keep the people safe, sometime in the midst of all that was happening, someone had the bright idea that if God said we should avoid something then maybe it would be a good idea not to have anything to do with whatever it was at all. This idea grew and before you knew it there were things being added and taken away util instead of a fence the people were now in prison. God's perfect instructions that told us what we could do were now outside of another fence, a man made fence of more rules. Much like the Constitution of the United States used to be the supreme law of the land but now we have a myriad of more laws before we can get to the Constitution, that is how the Torah became. What began as a few instructions so easy a seven year old could understand them was surrounded by a legal system that was useful only to a select few. One of the few things that didn't change much was the dietary laws and that is practically the same among the Jewish community today. So why do modern Bible believing Christians eat things that are not considered food? The answer is easy but to get to it we need to do some digging.

We can begin with Matthew 15 and Mark 7, this is the same incident told by 2 writers. While the disciples were eating bread in an obviously kosher Jewish setting, the Pharisees didn't question what was being eaten. Certainly bread can be eaten without worrying if is is clean or unclean, the only time we consider bread is during the feast of uneven bread. During this feast no leavening is to be used to bake but this was not the situation in these 2 passages. The pharisees question was why didn't the disciples wash their hands before they ate the bread, today that may seem obvious to wash before we eat but this was different, this was a ritual hand washing and not done to kill germs. In fact if the disciples would have been eying fruit or meat there would have been nothing said at all because the hand washing was only for bread. (Remember what I said about adding to the Torah?) Y'shua had instructed the disciples to violate the Pharisee rules about hand washing; Y'shua did not instruct the disciples to violate God's instructions. Initially, this conversation had nothing to do with food it dealt with is man's law more important than God's law. The verse which Y'shua said it's not what god in us that defiles us but what comes out has been twisted to mean anything other than what this lesson is about. The food we eat is processed physically, our actions and our speech is processed spiritually, so the bread we eat doesn't make us impure, our sinful actions and speech make us impure.

If you still think these passages are about food, look at the earliest manuscripts and you will find that there are some things missing from what we read today. There are a few translations of the Bible which add in parentheses that Y'shua made all food clean and that is not even in the early English translations so clearly someone is using their editing power to lead others away from what was originally written. So if there are people who are willing to edit the Bible to suit themselves are they conveying the true word of God? probably not and I will get to that later. But for now on to Acts Chapter 10.

In Acts 10 clearly Peter has a vision, in verse 10 we learn he was in a trance.

What occurred in this vision, dream or trance whichever we choose to name it is extremely important to Peter. God shows Peter something 3 times (bear in mind that sometimes it is hard to get through to Peter) some type of cloth is lowered and Peter is told to 1, get up then 2, kill and 3, eat. So before we look at what was on the cloth Peter is told to take some type of action, now there were only animals on the cloth, there was nothing else. Naturally Peter refuses to eat anything that God has instructed him not to eat, but why? wasn't this God speaking to him in his vision? If Peter was certain that God was telling him to eat what was on the cloth and he was hungry isn't it possible that he would have eaten what God was placing in front of him? There have been sermons preached and books written all about how to interpret Peter's dream but we don't need to interpret the dream because Peter gives us the interpretation himself in verse 28 when he tells Cornelius you know it is against Jewish law (not Torah) for a Jew to associate with someone who is not a Jew. But God had shown me(where? in his vision) that I should call no *person* unholy or unclean.

Peter was told first to get up and he woke up from the trance, secondly to kill, he killed the pharisee law that he could not go with the men sent to him by Cornelius and third he ate, Peter took into his self that he would do what God asked him to do and that wasn't eating animals that were not considered food. So again we have misinterpretation and misconception leading us to believe something that isn't true and is inconsistent with Biblical Authority. There is nothing in any of the verses which we read concerning food that anything was ever changed, even the dietary instructions are completely consistent with Biblical authority throughout the Bible.

Now that the we have a definition of what food is in the Bible and an explanation of the way that some people try to twist scripture to suit their own agenda, it should be reasonable to conclude there remain some animals we do not consider food. I could use the culture argument as well which compares the things we eat in the United States that are considered delicacies in other parts of the world such as dog, monkey or rat. Of course no discussion of this topic would be complete without mentioning there is no punishment for eating unclean food but if you touch an the carcass of an unclean animal you will be unclean until sundown. Why is there no punishment for eating unclean animals? because there may come a time when that is the only thing to eat and preservation of life is far more important than starving to death when there is a tabby cat sandwich within reach. Don't overlook the promise we have from God that if we follow His instructions He will provide for us, so we should expect that if we do things His way we won't need to worry about eating Tabby, Fido or Arnold.

What about the wine? if we're going to eat we need to have something to drink, right? Examining this is going to be interesting because just as the Pharisees added to the Torah basically instituting Jewish law, there are many denominational churches which done the same with alcohol. I need to be very careful and not downplay the danger of wine and other alcohol but at the same time correcting the confusion about exactly what the Bible reveals about it as well. The major difference can be found when we compare church doctrine with scripture and remember when we do this that Biblical Authority is the standard and not church doctrine. Let's begin with our standard, the Bible.

The first time we encounter the word wine in scripture is in Genesis 9:21 when Noah had processed the grapes he had grown after leaving the ark. After consuming too much something major happened because we see in verse 24 that after Noah awoke from his wine he knew what Cain had done to him so obviously this was no small event. In this passage the lesson is that too much wine has may lead to a negative outcome. Yet the next time we see the word wine is in Genesis 14:18 when Melchizedek or the Malke Zeddec as it is pronounced in Hebrew, meaning king of righteousness brings the bread and wine to Abraham. This is important because this is the incident where Abraham learns the blessing which he passes down to his family that reveals the coming Messiah as shown in the bread and the wine. The blessing begins; Blessed are you Yehovah, our God king of the universe, who brings forth bread from the earth. The blessing for the wine begins the same way;

Blessed are you Yehovah, our God king of the universe, creator of the fruit of the vine. Y'shua in John 8:56 said that Abraham rejoiced to see his (Y'shua's) day, this is where Abraham had that experience. The Hebrew language is self defining, Abraham would have known exactly what the blessing was for and so he insisted that his family recited the same blessing each time bread and wine are served and that continues to this day in most Jewish homes. I need to make sure you get the difference here, this is not specifically a Jewish blessing, and it isn't a blessing for the bread and wine either. This blessing is for God and is the same blessing Y'shua would have used every time bread or wine was served even at the last supper. He didn't bless the bread he blesses the Father who provides the bread and the wine. The Father provides the supreme sacrifice and the Father also provides the blood which pays the price for our violation of the blood covenant at Mount Sinai. WE can see now that wine in this circumstance has a positive outcome, after ll what could be more positive than Y'shua once again offering that blessing when he raises a glass at the marriage supper of the lamb.

Some may be asking "What about Leviticus 10:9?" and that is a legitimate question. throughout Leviticus instructions are given to Moses who is to speak those instructions to certain people or groups. Not each of God's instructions are for everyone, some are for men, some for women, some for children or animals and some specifically for the levite priests and sometime just for those who are serving in the Tabernacle. Leviticus 10:9 is slightly different, God speaks directly to Aaron, and tells him not to drink wine or strong drink when they go into the tabernacle. This prohibition is for specific people doing specific jobs in a specific place not for the average person then or now. Many churches twist this combined with Paul's first letter to timothy in chapter 3 where there is a list of attributes for a person desiring a higher place in the leadership of a fellowship but they completely ignore chapter 5 verse 23 which reads don't drink water but a little wine for the stomach's sake. Again we begin to see how church doctrine strays from Biblical Authority, more importance is placed on the rules of the church than are place on scripture. This is exactly what the Pharisees were doing near the end of these second Temple, implementing so many rules the people thought they were in prison because they couldn't get close to the fence that was God's instructions for their lives. Today people want to shout legalism when the hear someone wants to follow God's instructions while they at the same time try to enforce their man made doctrine onto every one else proudly proclaiming; "You can't get into Heaven unless you live our way!"

According to Paul, someone in a leadership position of an assembly of believers should not get drunk. That is sound advise and based on the Leviticus 10 instruction but does Paul imply those in leadership or anyone else should abstain from alcohol? certainly not because that would be inconsistent with the rest of the Bible. What about the people who are not leading a church or who are simply part of the community? God gives us certain times which He has set aside for us to celebrate. These feasts are outlined in Leviticus 23 and although many people today view them specifically as "Jewish" feasts they are not. Our Creator never relinquished ownership of these appointed times and when we read what is written in Leviticus 23 we plainly see these are the feasts of who? Most Bibles use the 2 words The LORD, specifically God, our Creator, He alone owns these celebrations and uses them as rehearsals to reveal to us His plans. The crucifixion and resurrection of Y'shua perfectly matches the Passover, unleavened bread and first fruits feast and those are the only tools that John uses to show others in his gospel account who Y'shua is. These appointed times are so important that our Creator assigned the sun, the moon and the stars as a calendar to tell us when to celebrate them before He created Adam. The word translated as seasons in Genesis 1:14 is the same word translated as feasts in Leviticus 23:2, the Hebrew (מידעומ) pronounced "moh-a-deem" meaning appointed times. Unfortunately this doesn't maintain the continuity in English which may be one of the reasons modern Christians refuse to acknowledge God's appointed times.

The explanation for the feasts was necessary to explain Deuteronomy 14; in this chapter Moses is reminding us what food is and then speaks about when every man was to go to the place where God chooses to put His name. Moses is speaking about the times that every man was to go to what would eventually be Jerusalem, and he tells us that if it is too far to travel with your tithes (the products of your agricultural work) then you are to sell those things and take the money and purchase what you need to celebrate. Here you are allowed ox, sheep, wine, strong drink or whatever your soul desired. Abstinence from alcohol was not in God's instructions for His appointed times and we see it was also to be used in the service at the Tabernacle and in the Temple. The use of wine and other alcoholic beverages was never condemned but there are warnings about overindulgence. While intoxication itself is not sin, it has the potential to remove that self discipline to follow God's instructions which leads to sin. In other words, getting drunk is not the sin, it is the sinful acts you do when you are drunk that you may not ordinarily do if you were sober that are the sin. The modern church doctrines that prohibit the use of alcohol are designed to prevent the possibility of sin because you may not be using good judgement if you drink too much. These doctrines are not based on Biblical Authority they instead have their foundation in the minds of people trying to control force their will on others.

When we choose to use the Bible as the standard by which we hold everything else accountable including ourselves, then we have a far greater opportunity to please our Creator. We are designed to live long, healthy, productive successful and happy lives when we follow His instructions. Maintaining Biblical Authority ensures that follow those instructions to the best of our ability with the information we have available at the time. There will always be unanswered questions about some details that have been lost through mistranslation, tradition, doctrine or some other infusing force but when we strive to do the best we are able to do and the most we have with the resources we have available then if we fall slightly short of our goal God's mercy and His grace will make up the difference.

CHAPTER 6

OVER AND OVER we find things that have been taught about the Bible or religion that are not consistent with Biblical Authority. Children's Bible stories and songs are not even safe from those who want to influence young minds, Jeremiah 16:19 reads in part that our father's have inherited lies. If our father's were given lies are they to be blamed of their failure to examine them? Are we any less guilty? today we have the information to search thousands of documents in just a few seconds, we have more information both written and exhumed archeological artifacts than any previous generation and yet we still cling to tradition and doctrine above the Bible. When Y'shua said follow me and I will make you fishers of men he wasn't saying anything new. Jeremiah 16 God tells us he will scatter the children of Abraham then in verse 16 He says that He will send fishers for them and then he will send hunters to search out the mountains and the caves. Yet that very important lesson isn't even part of the children's song Fisher's of Men.

Another children's song is about a boy named David and a little sling, this gives us an image of David maybe 10 or 12 years old trying to fight Goliath. David had already killed a bear and a lion when he went to deliver supplies to his brothers who were fighting the Philistines. Also we read that King Saul was head and shoulders above any other man, meaning he was physically a large person, would Saul have offered David his armor if it would not have even come close to fitting him? this should send a big red flag to tell us that David himself was a large man. These are real people we read about, the king of a nation at war would not entertain the thought of a child going into battle and would not offer armor unless it would fit.

We need to purge our minds of the fairy tales we have when we listen to mere Bible stories and reset our thinking to learning the lessons that are revealed. Daniel thrown into the lions den is another example of misguided thinking because many people have the idea that he was a young man and the Babylonians actually picked him up and threw him into a pit of hungry lions. While that does sound exciting and dangerous, it simply didn't happen that way and the reason for Daniel getting locked in with the lions becomes lost or forgotten amid the stimulating story. Daniel had been governor under 4 kings which would have made him much older than the pictures we see, When Darius passed the decree that no one was to pray to any god or any man except the king. Daniel went to his room and opened a window to pray and was overheard by Daniel's enemies who reported it to the king. The question in our mind today should be why did Daniel open the window and pray so they could hear him? (more about that in another chapter)

Believe it or not but the Bible has been the victim of Christmas carols for years. Yes Christmas carols have added so much confusion that many people have placed more importance in the music than in the real story of the

Earthly birth of the Messiah. The reality is there was no drummer boy, no cattle lowing, no wise men, and no jingle bells or Santa Clause at the birth of Y'shua. None of these things can be found in Scripture and the word Christmas be found in the Bible either.

To clear up any confusion I am remaining faithful to Biblical Authority for this explanation of Christmas, what is really in the Bible without the traditions to get in the way. The Christian Christmas as celebrated on December 25 is derived from the Roman sun-god celebration of Saturnalia a pagan deity just like all of the other pagan sun-gods who were born as the daylight began to lengthen again. Their names are many and varied with the culture and language as they came out of Babylon after the destruction of the tower and the confusion of language which God used to disperse the people all over the world. Their rituals remained similar as did the other portions of their celebrations including orgies and child sacrifice. Saturnalia was the largest Roman celebration of the year according to some reference books but was certainly a large and important celebrations at the very least. So the first quest would be why would the Roman's require the lowly Jew's to register during A Roman Holiday? That simply didn't make any sense so we should look and find what the Bible reveals about the birth of Y'shua.

Most people would go to Luke 2 and read about the birth itself but to find the formula for the time of birth we should go to Luke 1. Luke informs us that he actually understands what he has witnessed and the things he didn't witness personally were told to him by the people who were there at the time. In other words Luke is telling us he is a reliable witness to the events he is describing. He begins in verse 5 to lay out the timing for the birth of Y'shua by giving us the timing for the birth of John the Baptist, the son of Zacharias the priest. Luke reveals that Zacharias was in the Temple when the order of the Abia priests were there and according to 2 Chronicles 23; 6 David divided the courses of the priests. 2 Chronicles 24; 10 records that the corse of Abija was the eighth course of priests to serve. With Zachrias in the Temple in Jerusalem about 10 weeks into the year which began in the spring because Passover is in the beginning of months (Exodus 12; 12) that would mean he was serving near the time of Shavuot, what would become Pentecost on the modern church calendar. Zacharias has a conversation which leaves him deaf and unable to speak (dumb and unable to speak are the same thing, this is a mistake in the King James translation) he then returns home and Elisabeth becomes pregnant with John. Even with miracles in the Bible, it still requires 9 months of time from conception to birth so John would have been born in the spring go the year. Why is this important you ask? because we know that the Mary went to visit her cousin Elisabeth she was 6 months pregnant with Y'shua, Luke 1; 36. Which is really quite interesting because that would place the time of the conception of Y'shua around if not during Chanukah, the Feast of Dedication which celebrates when the Temple was rededicated after the Greeks were defeated and before the Roman invasion.

With this information we can be reasonably certain that Y'shua was actually born in the fall of the year quite probably on the first day of Sukkot, the Feast of Tabernacles. as John writes the word became flesh and tabernacled among us. Also there is evidence that during the time of Y'shua's birth there would have been around 1 million men required to go up to Jerusalem for each of the feasts. This is a perfect time to have each register for the census that was taken and allowed the Romans their Holiday without interruption from the Jewish people. The plains of Bethlehem where the lambs for the Temple service were born in the spring would have been a fine place for the men to build their sukkot. The shepherds would have moved the flocks out and away from their regular fall grounds to the hill country where they could be close enough to be near Jerusalem for the feat but also near the flocks which they were responsible for.

Luke 2; 12 has the angels telling the shepherds to search for a visible sign, something so out of place they can't miss it. A baby not born in a home where children would be born, but in a sukkah, the lamb of God born in the fall of the year exactly where the lambs were born in the spring for the Temple services. Imagine the Shepherds walking through that village of temporary dwellings searching for a newborn baby. That was something that wasn't done either, Leviticus 12; 2 instructs that if a mother gives birth to a male child she is unclean for 7 days. That doesn't mean she is dirty for 7 days it is a time for her to be alone and bond with the child. The blood lost during childbirth is important as well, and there must be a time of rest and mourning for the lost life that was in the blood even though there is a new life to care for. So no one would have normal been to visit a newborn baby boy until after the mother's time of uncleanliness was finished. The shepherds being told to search for the baby was a sign for them and having the shepherds come that night was a sign for Mary as she pondered these things in her heart,(Luke 2; 19).

So much has been overlooked when it comes to the birth of Y'shua because we would rather enjoy the traditions we have been taught. Read Luke chapter 2 and look for any evidence of any animals mentioned in the lesson.

Most people have a picture of poor little Mary riding side-saddle on a donkey going to Bethlehem, the problem is that is not in the Bible. We are told that Joseph took Mary with him and went to be counted and taxed, we are told when this happened and we are all told that any of the homes where Mary would have usually stayed were full. Any first or second century person who lived in that area would have known when they went and why, and they would have understood why there was no room in town for Mary. Basically it was tourist season in Jerusalem, everyone was there for the feast. Now here we are 2,000 years later trying to understand a culture we are not familiar with and we wonder why we are confused and think there are con-tradictions in the Bible.

Even the Greek language isn't much help here, the word translated into English as manger is a completely different word than what the Greek Septuagint uses for Sukkot. Even though the Greek word describes a tempo-rary shelter it is mostly used for animals which is why we have the tradition of animals at the nativity. No animals are recorded by Luke though, and since he claims to be a reliable witness we should believe his record. The word manger conjures up the thought in our 21st century mind of a place where animals feed but in the days of large sailing ships a manger was a covering for the lines with which the bow of the ship was mored. So imagine a sailor on the may-flower bringing the pilgrims to the new world and hearing the story for the first time her the baby was laid in a manger. They would be wondering how he got on a ship to begin with but their first thought would not have been a feed trough. This is why we need to be diligent when studying the scripture, we need to be able to separate the traditions we have learned from the truth using Biblical Authority.

From songs to art to literature to legend to tradition to church doctrine, the birth of Y'shua has undergone an evolutionary sequence of man made trappings which confuse and confound the most astute Bible scholar. No person and no resource denies that the traditional timing and trimming that surround Christmas have pagan origins but everyone seems to proclaim that we have "Christianized" Christmas. Well if it is that easy why not Christianize orgies, illegal drugs and murder? Deuteronomy 12 reminds us 2 ties in the same chapter that we are not to learn the way of the pagan. We are not to use pagan celebrations to worship our Creator, he call it an abomination. we have become so arrogant that we are smarter than God, using the things He calls disgusting to praise Him. All the while we proclaim the pagan aspects don't mean anything to me. Sadly, we don't get to choose what the pagan aspects mean to us, we are not smarter than God and we are not God, it is what those things mean to *Him* that matter, not to us. His universe, His rules.

What about the wise men, the magi from the east? were they at the manger the night Y'shua was born? no they were not. These wise men were Chaldean astronomers, descendants of the Babylonians which Daniel would have taught. They kept careful records and recognized the conjunction of stars which Daniel told them to look for. After seeing the star and gaining travel permission the distance from Babylon to Jerusalem was well over 500 miles of traveling. I highly doubt they would have jumped on a plane and been there any time close to the time of the birth. Even Matthew 2; 11 record them entering a house which helps put this lesson in perspective. After the feast of Tabernacles, Joseph and Mary presented the child in the Temple and went home to Nazareth where the wise men found them.

How many wise men found the baby? we don't know. There are 3 gifts mentioned, gold, frankincense and murre. Would only 3 scientist travel over 500 miles alone through the desert with a kings ransom? Most probably a small caravan with several soldiers accompanied the wise men to make certain their gift was delivered in tact. Does this give a different concept of the nativity? using Biblical Authority to understand these lessons often reveals something quite different than what we have been told.

When we remember the people in the Bible were real people living real lives and not some group of magical mythical beings then we should have a better understanding of the way they lived. They ate, slept and studied as well as going about their daily lives much as we do today. They even used the latest technology that they had access to and could afford. Putting all of this together and using Biblical Authority we have a much better concept of when Y'shua was born, who was there and we have a reliable witness to tell us that he wasn't born in a borrowed stable but in a temporary shelter, a sukkah carefully constructed by Joseph. Our Creator began orchestrating the birth of Y'shua before Adam was formed and we owe Him our time to carefully study so we properly understand how we are to worship Him and serve Him. Not on some pagan date but on our Creator's time, when He asks us to worship Him.

When we read the Bible there is nothing to indicate that we are to celebrate the birth of Y'shua but that doesn't mean we should't either. I would suggest if we celebrate that we should do it when it actually happened and not on some pagan holiday. As for the giving of gifts, yes it's nice to give and receive as well but if you really want to give your family or friends something nice that you want them to have, why wait for a pagan celebration? give it to them because you love them while you have the opportunity to see their joy. We are not guaranteed tomorrow, and I know at least 2 people who have found Christmas gifts with their names on them after a parent and a spouse had passed away. Those people never had the chance to see the happiness on the faces of the people they loved but the ones who received the gifts had no joy because they could not share that joy with the person who gave the gift. We should strive to make each day special, go ahead and use the good china and silverware. Use the fancy glasses that made you feel happy when you acquired them, give the people you love the things you want them to have without waiting for a day when the world is celebrating the rebirth of the sun. Y'shua didn't wait to heal or forgive, he made everyday about doing something for others, using the skills the Father gave him to make life better for others and we should follow his example.

CHAPTER 7

I'M OFTEN ASKED about worship, how should we worship, where should we worship, and somehow the questions always seem to come back to the sacrifices. The sacrifices were there as a reminder, a constant witness that we had broken a contract with our Creator. Worship had very little to do with the sacrifice so let's take a look at what worship is in the Bible. As we go back to Genesis, this time in chapter 2 verse 15 we see Adam was placed in the garden to tend and keep it. The word tend here has more than one meaning as many Hebrew words may but this is quite interesting because of the context not only in this verse but in future verses as well. Here we have the Hebrew word הדבעל (le-bey-dah) which has been translated as tend, cultivate, make salves and believe it or not, worship but what does worship have to do with cultivating a garden and slavery? The way the word is conjugated or the way the surrounding words are used has the ability to change the context of the word but the intent of the word remains the same. When we use the skills our Creator gives us to build His kingdom, we are actually performing a type of worship. The word for keep in theirs verse is the Hebrew word הרמשל (la-show-mare) which also means to guard.

Adam was instructed not just to work the garden but to make his work worshipful as he guarded the garden.

How is this helpful when we think about worship today? our modern concept of worship focuses on either church, study or music but that really limits the time we worship in our minds. Our Creator designed each of us individually with certain skills that we are to use to benefit not only ourselves but the people around us as well. When we use those skills to benefit others, that is a form of worship just like if we were singing in a choir. God also gives us this instruction manual we call the Bible to help us know and understand how we are to use the skills He gives us. Although the Torah is the first five books of the Bible and there are many lessons to be learned the instructions that are there (that so many people get confused about) all point to the first ten command that God spoke at Mount Sinai. Later Y'shua would divide those into 2 categories being love God and love your neighbor. The rest of the instructions teach us how to apply those 10 things to our daily life. When we follow God's instructions we are worshiping Him, it's so simple a 7 year old hearing the Torah read for the first time could understand it and we have confused and twisted it to the point that people say it can't be done. If you really want to learn how our Creator chooses for us to worship Him, open your Bible and do the things it tells us to do and don't do the things it tells us not to do.

Worship shouldn't end when the church door closes behind you if you choose to believe the Bible instead of Church doctrine or tradition. Why then do so many preachers teach us that those things have been done away with? they don't hold the Bible above everything else. There are denominations built on single verses which ignore Biblical Authority and these are just as dangerous as the traps set by false teachers. Modern Christians proclaim that the "law" has been done away with but they fail to read Matthew chapter 5. Y'shua teaches his disciples (and only the disciples were there for the sermon on the mount) that he did not come to do away with the law he came to complete it and Heaven and earth would pass away before everything was completed. When we examine that statement we need to recognize that earth has not passed away, we're still here so not everything has been completed yet. This means that according to Y'shua the law still stands and we are still accountable to it. I actually has a pastor try to convince me that because Y'shua said this before the cross that things have changed after the resurrection. My response was a simple question,"So everything that Y'shua said and taught before the resurrection doesn't mean anything?" he couldn't get away from me fast enough.

If the law has been done away with how is John able to write in his first letter 3; 4 that sin is a transgression of the law? this is after not only the resurrection but the ascension as well. The arguments use to claim that God's instructions don't matter anymore do not withstand the scrutiny of Biblical Authority. Just because someone wants something to be true doesn't make it true and that means evolution, flat earth and our Creator's instructions all fall and stand when closely examined with Biblical Authority. We should realize the instructions are for our benefit not our punishment, our Creator designed us to live according to His instructions and that hasn't changed. Sin has corrupted our minds and our bodies and we probably today more than any other time in history are witness to the result of sin; disease, infirmity, mental health issues along with rebellious and selfish actions are just a few. But we refuse to see the real problem, the spirit behind the problem.

Modern Christians today are eager to proclaim how everyone needs to accept the Holy Spirit into their lives but they overlook a very real issue. If we are able to accept the Holy Spirit then we must be able to accept non-holy spirits as well. No one want to address this because when we do some people go on auto pilot and hear the words demon possession and that may or may not be accurate depending on the person and the situation. Back to Genesis 2:7 God breathed into Adam the breath of life and he became a living soul To be clear the animals have souls, but do not have the breath of life that allows us to communicate on a higher level. Animals communicate on a lower level of grunts, whistles and body language while humans speak and exchange ideas just like the heavenly beings we are made in the image of. Look at Psalm 82, our Creator is judging the other gods, clearly they did something to deserve what was coming to them. I'm using this example do demonstrate the difference between the spirit world and our physical world because 1 kings 22 wouldn't make any sense without understanding there is some type of council of spirits with our Creator in Heaven. In verses 21 and 22 we read that a spirit is willing to be a lying spirit in the mouth of a prophet of Ahab and our Creator grants the permission to make it happen. We need to understand and acknowledge there is a spirit world that interacts with our physical world.

Now that we have an understanding and Biblical proof that there are spirits which act under the authority of our Creator we could look at a well used passage to see there are spirits which do not come with the authority of our Creator but act on their own, often causing us much grief and pain. Matthew, mark and Luke record the inter-action between Y'shua and a man who had many spirits in him which is why together they were called legion. These spirits had the man living naked among the graves in the caves and as there were other men there some of which had the same kind of spirits we can speculate what these spirits were causing these men to do. The spirits recognized Y'shua and begged him not to send them away, as Y'shua allowed the spirits to transfer into a herd of pigs the pigs recognized and understood what was happening and knew it was better to drown in the river than live with these spir-its. This lesson demonstrates that we as humans sometimes allow the wrong spirit into our lives and that creation itself understands evil when it is put on it.

having Biblical foundation for being able to find both good and bad spirits interacting with people, (and there are many more witnesses in the Bible for each) we can now begin to examine how the spirits work, how to recognize them and what our response should be. We can begin by learning how these spirits work in our physical world, there is an example in Judges 6; 34 where in English it reads the Spirit of God came on Gideon. This is really a poor trans-lation because when read in Hebrew the concept is that Gideon was so willing to serve only the Creator that His Spirit put Gideon on and wore him like a coat. I previously used the example from 1 Kings 22 where the spirit enters the mouth of a prophet and there are numerous other places we read about interaction of spirits in the physical world we live in. These spirits when they are present guide our actions and influence our response to information. A good example would be the spirit of addiction; addiction will guide us to whatever substance that the spirit desires. Sometimes it is drugs or alcohol and sometimes pornography or other sexual pleasure and sometimes it guides us to an overwhelming amount of information stimulation which occurs when we can't seem to watch enough news of other type of media. Here is where we need to be careful and understand the person which this spirit resides often doesn't know the spirit is living in them because the persons action reflect the rest of the world they live in. Did you catch that? many spirits are camouflaged to look like the world we live in.

So if these spirits are familiar, how do we know they are there? The litmus test is reasonably easy, is the person in question following our Creator's instructions? Be careful because sometimes it may seem we are doing what God wants us to do but instead of serving in such a way that God gets the glory we brings fame to ourselves. That is the lesson in Matthew 25, Even though the people may have been visiting the prisoner or feeding the hungry or even healing the sick; who received the thanks and the praise? When we do these things to show how righteous we are then we are claiming God's glory for ourselves which is why Y'shua tells them to leave his presence. Why does God allow selfish people to do good works in His name? because the ones receiving the food, visit or healing need it, but the ones who offer these things not because they want to see our Creator glorified but have a desire to claim the thanks and praise for themselves don't have a heart to know God.

Believe it or not when we are following our Creator's instructions we greatly diminish the opportunity to become selfish. His instructions are designed to keep our minds first on Him second on those around us and lastly ourselves. The spirit of jealousy has the ability to cover the eyes of far too many people because sin makes it difficult for us to watch someone else succeed even when we truly want the too. Deep down in our hearts we want to see the people who deserve recognition be rewarded for their efforts but there is often that spirit of jealousy lingering just below the surface which causes us to sneer; maybe just for a second until we get it under control but if we're honest we've all done it. This is why we hold ourselves and each other accountable, not judging our faith but judging our actions. These spirits of addiction, jealousy and others cause us to act in a way that contradicts Biblical Authority, so we are able to conclude when we act or speak in such a way that we are not following God's instructions we are following or allowing an unholy spirit to guide us, but when we do follow God's instructions we are following or allowing the Holy Spirit of our Creator to be our guide.

When we observe people through the viewpoint of Biblical Authority and not tradition, church doctrine or what we might think is right we can see which spirit is guiding their life. I knew a man years ago who was able to defeat the spirit of addiction and to prevent himself from allowing back into his life he changed the rout he took to and from work every day because he didn't want to be tempted back into the same barroom where he first met that spirit. After several months he needed to past there one day and because he had replaced the spirit of addiction and allowed the Holy Spirit to guide him, he didn't even notice the doorway into that bar. He now had the ability to walk down that street and not pay any attention to that place. He eventually got to the place where he could have a glass of wine with dinner without the worry of having that spirit of addiction wanting back into his life. Because he began to follow his Creator's instructions he was able to regain control of which spirit he would follow. Modern Christians are quick to proclaim that Y'shua forgives sin but they hesitate to remember the "go and sin no more" portion, which means now go follow the creator's instructions.

The most difficult person to recognize an unholy spirit is is ourself. Often the someone wants corrects us we allow the spirit of anger or resentment to guide our actions. This should be our first clue that we are not following the Holy Spirit of our Creator. There is a time for anger and even a time for jealousy and God uses these spirits sometimes to guide us but when our first response to someone questioning our actions is defensive anger, we may actually need correcting. Again the test for this is not hard, it simply is finding where the Holy Spirit is in the situation and following it to build the Kingdom of Heaven instead of following an unholy spirit to tear it down. With prayer and practice to recognize which spirits you are following it doesn't take long to understand the and see them in you life. As Paul said we don't fight against flesh and blood but against the spirits which try to lead us away from our Creator.

We can think of spirits as emotions, even though we think of addiction as being physical, many addictions begin as emotional dependance. anger is an emotion, how we act on that anger is the physical manifestation of the emotion. Doctors are now telling us that stress can lead to many different physical ailments, believe it or not, not forgiving someone is a form of stress. The spirits we allow into our life will determine how healthy we are. If the fruit of the spirit are (some of the things) as Paul puts it in Galatians 5; 22 love, peace patience, gentleness, goodness, kindness and self control, these are the physical manifestations of these emotions. For someone with the spirit of addiction to defeat that spirit, they will need to first recognize it and physically speak directly to it and tell it to leave their body, leave their home and leave this world. The next step is to understand how the Holy Spirit will replace that spirit which you just evicted. Sometimes this is an immediate circumstance and sometimes it is not, there are some variables which we need to know, first and foremost how honest are we when we evict that spirit? we may not want the bad situations it causes but do we really want it gone? if we are not completely honest with ourself and our creator that spirit will know it and fight to stay. Remember we are dealing with our own desires in these situations and sometimes the hardest person to be honest with is ourself. Once we have been completely open and honest and can proclaim there will be no room for whatever spirit we are evicting that is when our Creator will fill that vacancy with His Holy Spirit. Again depending on how long the unholy spirit was living there a fight will probably take place and it may be necessary to adjust your lifestyle as well. there may be some people who would try to bring you back to where you just left because their spirits miss the one you just evicted and they want you back as well. Don't give up and don't give in, it can be a hard fight but when you choose our Creator He will win.

We should have an understanding of what a spirit is and how to recognize is and defeat it. You may be wondering what the difference is between a spirit and a demon and first we need to define what a demon is. Many people if they had to describe a demon would probably offer some version of an artists drawing or describe something they saw in a movie. Don't worry as much about what they look like as what they can do. Demons have the ability to physically manifest themselves into our physical world and that makes them very dangerous. they can and do often reside in our physical bodies sometimes without our knowledge. Demons if left unchecked long enough learn to control the person they are living in. So to define a demon it is; something from the spiritual world with the ability to enter our physical world and influence the lives of people. Demons do not always need to live in the body of a person but will if they find someone who is willing to allow them to.

Notice that I keep explaining that both spirits and demons can only live in us if we allow them to, we have the ability and the authority to choose what resides in our body. When we choose to be obedient to our Creator the unholy spirits and the demons can not stay. Just as 1 John 1:5–10 describes that darkness can not be in the presence of light, then evil will leave a person when they begin to follow God's instructions and do what is right. (from Ezekiel 18) The choice of our actions is ours to make, we can not depend on the old saying "The devil made me do it" as a defense for our actions.

Understanding this we can now understand how to deal with demons. Because they are a physically manifested being from the spirit world most people are right to be afraid of them. If you don't have the faith to acknowledge them or the courage to confront them it would be wise to find someone who has these abilities. Following Biblical Authority we know it is best to confront these beings on when they are not on their property. In 1 Samuel 26 David uses a strange phrase about being driven away from the LORD's inheritance to serve other gods. At first it is hard to understand but when we realize that David is no longer in the promised land it makes sense. If David had crossed the property boundary then he was subjected to those other gods. Today we know that we have the ability to mark territory and proclaim it for our Creator. By anointing the boundary markers with oil and proclaiming everything that we own, lease or rent we will use to build God' s kingdom, we are making His territory. Unholy spirits and demons are much easier to defeat when we are on ground that has been declared to be used for our Creator. Be careful not to confuse this with what is called consecrated ground as in a cemetery, I'm not introducing church rituals here. What I am meaning is property that people have control over which has been marked and the prayer made that as long as we have control, it will be used to glorify and uphold our Creator.

The first step to defeating and evicting a demon is very similar to defeating a spirit. Speak in a normal voice directly to God asking for His help with this. It doesn't need to be fancy or "churchy" the Bible tells us the disciple's we not fancy or churchy people. The spoken prayer releases our breath into the physical world which interacts with the spirit world and gives our Creator permission to intervene. I know some might be asking about silent prayer and I will get to that in another chapter but for now think of our creator right there with you and you are speaking to Him because He can hear you. Tell Him your desire to evict the spirit or demon or both that does not come from Him and replace that with His Holy Spirit to guide you. Don't allow yourself to think there will not be a fight or an argument at the very least. Remember the most important part is to trust your Creator, follow His instructions and if you need to distance yourself from some of the people who want that demon back then stay away from them. The most important part now is that God gets the glory, praise and honor. you didn't do it on your own and the best way to honor your Creator is by continuing to follow His instructions.

Some might think that I have oversimplified defeating a spirit or demon but there is nothing in the Bible that would indicate it is difficult. We have the ability to defeat them and the authority as well. Devils on the other hand are different. We often think of Satan as being the Devil because over the years the church has not acknowledged the link to the spirit world properly. For what ever reason the art world has added confusion and the movie and television industry has given us their interpretation also. Satan as described in the Bible is an adversary, something which works to defeat God and us as well. There has been much confusion about who Satan is and is his name Lucifer and how that all fits together. To put this simply, Lucifer occurs 1 time in the King James Bible, the Hebrew word that it is translated from is לליה (halal) and means shining. It has been translated as day star or shining one depending on the translator. There are figures of speech contained in the Bible that were used during the times of writers, we should not be confused or trapped by these figures of speech. Simply because someone referred to an enemy as brilliant doesn't mean they are as bright as the sun, it could easily mean they are smart enough to be dealt with carefully.

To move on, Devils have a desire to live vicariously through humans. Since they have nonemotional attachment of their own they invade the week and the willing to live their lustful and indulgent existence through people. That is why Y'shua said these can only be removed through prayer and fasting. He may not have been referring to food in that statement, fasting from whatever that particular Devil wants would render it weak. In other words if a Devil has a desire for pedophilia, preventing that action would weaken it and if the person wanted to be released, it would be possible when the Devil is weak and vulnerable. This is why we see pedophiles who have been in prison claim to be cured, the Devil that is in them is weakened and the real person is able to control themselves. The problem is if that person has no desire to be released from that Devil or the person doesn't repent and follow God's instructions the Devil will gain strength and take over if they are released form prison and it will seek it's gratification again. This example is best observed through the desire for blood, we have many records now of what we call serial killers. These people are bound to a devil with a blood lust, they kill for enjoyment and the people are seldom if ever given the chance to be released from that Devil. That doesn't mean that any of these people should be released from prison one they are incarcerated but it does mean we have the responsibility to release them from the bonds of their Devil.

By starving the Devil of it's desires it becomes weak and the control over the person is easier to break. Too often we fail to recognize that it may be a Devil guiding a person but we should remember at the same time that the person had a choice in the beginning to follow God or the Devil that guides them this is why they should remain incarcerated, it was their choice to follow that Devil when the lust began. Society has a responsibility to care for the person and give them the help they need but must also be careful to make examples so that others make the best choices. I asked the question at a meeting, "do you not murder because you may wind up in jail or do you not murder because God instructs us not to? The answers might surprise you, Most people agree not going to jail is a good thing, almost a fringe benefit of not committing murder but some stopped short of agreeing that we don't murder because of God's instructions.

If a person has a true desire to be released from a devil they must deny that devil of it's lusts. Weaken it to the point that it is vulnerable and then the real person is able to come back and speak to the Creator and working together they defeat that Devil and send it back to where it came from. Others may be able to guide that process but the desire of the person who is bonded to that Devil must be made known. No one else can release someone who has no desire to be healed, Matthew 17; 21 but this kind only goes out with prayer and fasting, others may be able to assist once a cry for freedom is made but the person afflicted must want to be free.

As we examine spirits, demons and Devils, we learn much about the way our world is affected by the spirit world. Paul was right we fight against the things we don't see. The examples are in the Bible, from spirits entering into the mouth of a prophet to get the response God desires from a king to Devils using people to fulfill their fantasies, our world is a battleground. Understanding how the 2 worlds interact is crucial if we truly want the greatest relationship we can have with our Creator. When our desire is to be as close to our Creator as possible and follow his instructions, living he way we are designed to live that is when the unholy spirits, demons and Devils try to drive a wedge between God and us. After all why would they waste their time with someone who doesn't care about God or who is already following their evil ways. Some may think they are being tested and in a way they are but it is not our Creator who is testing us when we choose Him it is those unholy things that are temping us to follow them.

The lessons we learn in Job are a wonderful example of this but too often are overlooked. The Bible reveals that Job was a righteous man who had a great relationship with God. Our Creator offers Job not because He wanted to test Job but because He trusted Job to remain faithful. Satan was convinced that the only reason Job was faithful was because God had blessed Job with many earthly things, (remember Job was a very rich man) and would deny his Creator if those things were taken away. Job understood that trust works both ways and remained faithful and was rewarded abundantly for it. Job was even granted an additional 20years of life (in Genesis 6; 3 we are only granted 120 years of life as a maximum) and Job was also rewarded with more wealth that he had before. Our Creator wants us to trust Him the same way Job trusted, that is a completely fulfilling relationship. Trust really is a 2 way street, if our only desire to have a relationship with God is for Him to keep giving and us to keep taking that is not a healthy relationship. Just like interaction between people, trust is something that must be present for a relationship to work. A marriage can't last if one person continues to display actions that violate the marriage vows and our Creator is asking for the same respect. Repeated throughout the Bible is the phrase "If you will hear My voice and obey my commands," in other words if we would be faithful then so will He.

We don't have a detailed description of Heaven or the spirit realm because we don't live there, we live on this earth in our physical universe. We do get small glimpses or snapshots from time to time which reveal just enough to make us even more curious but our concern should focus on how those things interact with and affect our world. We should be observant enough to understand when we are in a shadow and not directly in the light of our Creator because that is when something is trying to place itself between God and us. Job understood what was happening to him because he knew he had a choice to make, remain faithful and keep trusting God who was still there even though Job was in the shadow, or deny God and loose the light and be in complete darkness. Job's decision should be ours as well, remain faithful, even in a shadow we can still see but when there is no light at all and we are in complete and total darkness we are at the mercy of those unholy spirits and demons and Devils.

CHAPTER 8

We have examined and clarified many of the confusing passages and hopefully have discovered that all of the confusion is caused by our lack of knowledge and our failure to maintain Biblical Authority. In any kind of relationship, there needs to be open communication and our relationship to our Creator is no different. Most would agree that prayer is our main form of communicating with God, but we don't all agree on how this is should happen. Once again traditions and church doctrine interfere with our understanding of Scripture.

Many churches will at some time during their service have a time devoted to prayer and that is a good thing. Some churches have a tradition of reciting what is known as the Lord's prayer at some point during their service but do they really understand what that is? In Matthew chapter 6 Y'shua is teaching only his disciples at what is known as the sermon on the mount, he instructs them not to pray as the pagans do repeating the same empty and meaningless prayers but offers an example and in verses 9 through 15 we have what we call the Lord's prayer, the last verse by the way was added later because it is not in any of the early manuscripts which are available and is it missing from the Luke 11 teaching as well. This excellent example of a Hebrew prayer gives us an outline of how to approach God when we speak to Him. Even the opening our Father, causes us to think of God not just as a creator but as a member of a family. Remember what Y'shua teaching is in Matthew, don't use the same prayer repeatedly until it becomes meaningless. Our Creator, our Father wants us to speak to Him from our heart, He wants to hear our deepest desires and concerns and he wants to hear how much we love Him and trust Him. Our traditions have become exactly what Y'shua instructed us not to do, repeating the same prayer until it becomes meaningless to us, but because it comes from Him it will never be meaningless to God.

Some people seem to be afraid to pray, they think they are not good enough or don't have the right words and they think this because that is what they were taught. What a shame to think that we can't talk to the our Creator, even in the story of Pinocchio, the puppet is easily able to speak to the man who carved him out of wood. We should be encouraging people to speak to God instead of making them think their prayers are not good enough to be heard by God, by getting between someone and their Creator we cast that shadow, we become the wedge that drives apart, our intentions may be to help but our actions display something different. Sometimes we are uncertain of our words and sometimes we don't know how to explain our actions to God and that's ok because what He wants is to know that you don't have the words and something isn't well with you, in fact that's exactly when you need to be consulting Him and not ignoring Him.

Let's examine this thing we call silent or unspoken prayer, is there a Biblical principle for it or is it something that Satan is using to break the communication between God and man. Most people use Y'shua's words in Matthew 6; 6 when he instructs us to go into a closet to pray to justify silent prayer. The logic in using this verse to advocate for silent prayer is non existent. Why if you were instructed to think your prayer would there be a need to go into a closet where no one could hear you? Clearly Y'shua is not even hinting at being silent, he is saying that communication between you and your Heavenly father is personal and instead of making a mockery of prayer as some people were obviously doing, keep it personal. Just as every family has some things that are not public knowledge it is the same way with God's family. when we speak to God in private He will reward us openly in public, there are times when we need help from others but that was not the lesson in Matthew 6; 6.

The available research from the people who advocate for silent prayer reveals their misunderstanding of the way the spirit world affects our world. One way to look at spirit other than emotion is breath, God breathed into Adam. Because of this transfer of breath from God to man our speaking out loud releases a portion of our spirit into the physical world. That in turn connects us to God and has an affect on the spirit world and interaction on our behalf can then begin. there are several examples of this in Scripture. First let's look at Hannah, 1 Samuel records her not being able to have children and she was distressed about that. When she and her family were at one of the feasts she had eaten and had been drinking. Eli the priest watched her as she moved her lips but made no sound. He thought she was drunk and asked what she was doing. Hannah explained the wasn't drunk but upset and praying that God would allow her to have a child. Eli intervened on her behalf and spoke out in an audible voice to God. This example that a priest understood how to talk directly to our Creator and also as an intercessor for someone else is remarkable. We also learn that the priest had a desire for he prayer to reach the ears of our Creator and that happens when we speak in an audible tone.

Another example is in Daniel 6; 10, Daniel knew what the penalty was if he was caught praying to his God and not to the king but Daniel being obedient to our Creator prayed with the windows open. For Daniel to do this having the close relationship to God which he enjoyed, he must have understood more about prayer than we do today. There was a reason and a need for Daniel and Eli to speak their prayers to our Creator and that reason is connecting our spirit to the Holy Spirit through speech. Nehemiah is sometimes used as an example of silent prayer as he asks for help in front of the king. The problem with using these example is there is not enough information given to indicate it was silent. Nehemiah 2; 4 simply states that he prayed to God in Heaven, the speciation is that being in front of the king he would not have prayed out loud but we could just as easily speculate that he prayed a soft short prayer out loud. Again there just isn't enough information in this passage to make it a good example either way but since there are other prayers recorded we know that he did pray so that others could hear it often.

Psalm 139; 23 asks God to search our hearts and Jeremiah 12; 3 declares that our Creator knows the content of our heart. There are other example of this as well throughout the Bible and none of these verses are connected to communication. Time after rime we read that God knows our inner most thoughts and we know that is true but only through communication are we able to give

Him permission to intervene. our Creator will not force Himself into our life, He asks often for us to let Him in but He refuses to bust down the door and order us around. The choice is always ours if we follow His instructions or not One very important thing to keep in mind when testing our traditions and doctrine is we need to stay on the same track. if we are discussing prayer as communication then we need to look for verses that address communication. Verses such as Psalm 139; 23 and Jeremiah 12; 3 are true and used in their proper context are indeed very powerful but when we try to force those verses to mean something they are not designed to mean we loose the Biblical Authority and begin our own agenda. I read an article about silent prayer and how the writer was trying desperately to use it and improve it but couldn't. He discovered that trying to force our ideas and concepts into the Bible is futile. Our Creator designed this universe to work His way, His universe; His rules.

When we pray make it an open communication with our Creator, praise Him, Thank Him, worship Him and if necessary ask Him. Prayer is not a spiritual 911 call, we have no right to expect our Creator to come running to us when we get into trouble especially if we have been enjoying the actions that an unholy spirit or worse has been guiding us to do. In other words, if we have been having a good time sinning why would God help us until we are that we need to change our sinful ways" There is a small word that too many people forget, "if" you hear My voice and obey My commands the you will be my people and I will be your God. We must choose God before he will intervene for us and the only way to do that is through communication.

There are some people who can not speak for themselves, are they then condemned by our Creator? absolutely not! Just as Eli spoke on Hannah's behalf and intervened for her, we should follow his example. When we know someone can not pray for themselves it is our responsibility to intervene. We might not have all of the facts we need but God does and when we speak to Him for another and ask Him to get involved He will. The outcome might not be what we expect but it will not be our outcome, it will be God's. Moses spoke to God on behalf of an entire nation and God allowed a rebellious people to continue, imagine what would happen if every believer would ask our Creator to intervene on behalf of every unborn child or even if an entire church would intervene for just 1 member who was hurting. the power of prayer is staggering when we realize that we have an open line of communication with the creator of the universe.

I have been in churches where they entertain unspoken prayer requests, While I try to find a polite way to express my annoyance with this concept allow me to explain why. Many times there are no names used for these requests and while privacy is and needs to be a concern, if the person has a desire for some kind of intervention then that person needs to be honest and if the church they are surrounded by can not be trusted they need to find a different body of believers who can be trusted. Too often when these unspoken requests are made people look around with that "Well, we know what that means" look on their face and soon the gossip begins. If there truly is someone who needs intervention there should be people in the church who are available for such purposes. When a problem arrises which needs intervention the leadership of the church should be the first line of communication.

Today we have prayer chains and prayer lists in our churches but when we read the names on those lists they seldom change. When an entire church is truly praying for people those people should expect to receive healing or at least relief. Why are the people that many churches praying for not seeing results of prayer? primarily because they don't know how to pray. They might go through the motions but an honest conversation with the Father never happens and sometimes what they are asking for is not what God desires. David spent a long time fasting and praying for the life of his son recorded in 2 Samuel 12 but when the child died David washed and ate because he knew what God's answer was. Too many people have been trained to believe that God will give them anything they want and that can not be found anywhere in the Bible. When what we want contradicts what God wants, God will win every time. Isaiah 46:9–10 our Creator reminds us that He has told us the end from the beginning and he will do as He pleases.

So how are we as only created beings supposed to know what the Creator wants? we study His word and follow His instructions. The Bible is our instruction manual, given to us in small but very important sections over a long period of history. Contained in this book of books are the answers to all of our questions if we are willing to read what is written and do what the Bible instructs us to do. Our Creator communicating with us begins with Adam, he had a direct link to God until he and Eve rebelled. God spoke to many people and had conversations which are recorded in the Bible but today when we should realize how close we are able to be to our Creator we instead think He is too Holy, too distant or too busy for us. The very Creator who want to be involved with every aspect of our life from birth to our physical death on this earth proves repeatedly in the Bible that He is not too busy for us. God's love and concern for us is evident on every page of Scripture but we seem to be more concerned with our traditions and doing things our way than learning how our Creator designed us to be.

We believe the strangest things, we believe that the people in the Bible who spoke to God or who witnessed miracles were more than just human. We make up stories and try to pas them off as excuses for why we don't see the miracles we read about in the Bible. We are told that our Creator offers us a long, healthy, happy, successful and productive life if we follow His instructions and wonder why we don't witness those things. We think the age of healing miracles is over because we can't heal the sick or raise the dead. The phrase "Those things were for those people at that time" doesn't make sense when we read that we have the power to speak to our Creator and petition his intervention when we are doing things His way.

We are the biggest problem in our relationship to our Creator. We make bad choices, we want things that we are not created to have, we change our minds and follow the fantasies of the spirits that would guide us away from God. Yet among all of those distraction and all of that confusion, our Creator is standing firm, never changing, patiently waiting for us to repent and turn back to Him. We don't know how to ask our Creator for help in many situations because we don't truly know Him, we don't know what He expects from us because we believe what is easy and what we think because that is how we were trained to believe. Instead we should believe what is written in the Bible the way it was written because that is the way our Creator intended it to be. That is without the translation mistakes or the added personal agenda from an editor. If you really want to witness the power of prayer try asking for something that your Creator wants for you, try following His instructions for your life and see how your situation improves. That is not putting your Creator to the test that is testing yourself, it isn't testing God for us to do things His way. If you really want to witness answered prayer in a positive way, first repent, turn back to your Creator and learn to find His will in your life. Stop being the problem, life is much better when we learn how to do things God's way. Too many people can't understand why they are having such a difficult life when they are following an unholy spirit, they blame everything and everyone around them but have trouble understanding they are the problem.

Sometimes our Creator will allow us to become so desperate and so depressed that is seems we need to look up just to see the bottom side of down. For some people that is the only way they will ever realize that doing things their way doesn't work. Thankfully that is also when many will actually have their first open and honest talk with the Creator of the universe. I have spoken to many people who admit they thought they were a good person because of the way they lived, but it wasn't until they really opened up to God and had that moment of revelation that things begin to change. often some of the people who have this find a comfort zone, they try to meet God half way and think that is the best they can do. If they would just take the next step to find what their Creator really wanted for them they would be blessed beyond their wildest imagination and some people have a wild imagination.

I listened to a very sincere person one evening as they spoke about some things happening in the world. The comment that the church needed to come together and pray for direction was a really good place to begin. The problem becomes when we sit and pray and then fail to follow the instructions we are given. There is much more to a prayer meeting than sitting an begging God for what we want. We should be asking for us to see what He expects during these times of trouble. We have His instructions, when we ask for the understanding of how to apply those instructions the way He chooses for us to we no longer have the luxury of sitting on that safe church pew. When we view a prayer meeting much like a meeting of the board of directors or a staff meeting, when it is over we go to work. If we are still sitting and waiting after we have our instructions it appears that we don't want to follow those instructions. The people in the Bible didn't wait, the phrase "he rose early" is used several times to indicate a attitude of eagerness, even Abraham rose early when he took Issac to be sacrificed, (Genesis 22.) Sometimes we are given a job that we don't want to do but continuing to beg for a different outcome seldom is a good idea. We all sometimes ask our Creator if what He is saying to us really is what He wants but when we are obedient we go, we speak what we are given to speak or we do what we were given to do and then we receive the blessing. Remaining on the bench will never result in being blessed the way our Creator chooses to bless us. His Universe His rules.

CHAPTER 9

THERE IS WITHIN the Christian church today an attempt to define sin as anything other than what it is. When we discuss sin the definition needs to be clear and concise, many people choose to define sin as what separates us from God. That is not the definition of sin, separation from God is the result of sin. Adam and Eve's eviction from the garden was because of their action; their disobedience, they chose to eat the fruit which both of them knew they were told not to eat. Failing to follow our Creator's instructions is the Biblical definition of sin. 1 John 3:4 reads that sin is the transgression of the law. That is a Biblically poetic way to say that sin is not obeying God's instructions given to us through Moses. The "law" or the Torah are the instructions we find in the first five books of our Bible. So now that we have a definition of sin we can examine a commonly accepted axiom that we are born sinners, but does this conform to Biblical Authority? and if we are born sinners how is Y'shua able to command two people to "Go and sin no more"?

Psalm 51:5 has been commonly misread but not necessarily mistranslated, David writes that he was shaped in sin because his mother was a sinner even as she conceived him. This gets slightly confusing but when we really understand what David is trying to say so many other verses begin to make even more sense and we can get much more meaning from them. Think about what David writes this way, he was shaped, trained or taught to sin but by whom? he tells us that his mother was a sinner and that is the part of the statement that causes the confusion for us. We are not sinners because of our parents sin, Ezekiel 18 revels that the children are not responsible for the sins of the parents, each is responsible for their own self. So what David is really saying makes complete and perfect sense, his mother being a sinner taught him to sin.

We are not born sinners, to make this statement would require a belief that our Creator made us for evil purposes. Genesis 1:26 and 9:6 as well as many other places in Scripture like James 3:9 remind us we are made in God's image. Are we to consider that our Creator would make us in His own image in order for us be failures? certainly not! God gives us the free will because He wants us to make the choice to be obedient, He could have made us just like the animals and given us the instinct to live without the ability to communicate real thoughts and ideas but He didn't. God made us like Himself to a lesser degree, but an image of who He is. Just before He created man He looked at all of His creation and called it "very good" our Creator doesn't make anything bad in all of creation and we are no exception. Each of us according to Jeremiah 1:5 are formed by our Creator for a purpose. We can choose to follow that purpose or not, even Jonah chose not to go to Nineveh before he was convinced to obey God.

Psalm 139 David clarifies his description of being born a sinner, Verse 14 reads I know that I am fearfully and wonderfully made. In verse 15 David continues that God watches over him in his mother's womb, being carefully constructed. This doesn't read as though God was putting together a sinner, instead he was crafting perfection, adding the skills that David would use to defeat Goliath, outwit Saul and lead a nation. We are no different, God gives each of us certain skills which we are suited to. When we use those skills to benefit others we are blessed but when we try to ignore God's instructions and benefit only ourself we often fail. We are not born to sin we are trained to sin, we are born to live the way our Creator designed us to live, to care for creation and each other.

With that misconception clarified, now we can look at how and why Y'shua was able to Say to a man he healed and an adulterous woman "Sin no more." The man found in John chapter 5 spent 38 years lying beside a pool waiting and hoping to be healed. When Y'shua asks if he wanted to be healed the crippled man must have been thinking that this stranger would help him be first in the water when it bubbled. There was a belief at that time that when the water in the pool stirred or bubbled it was an angel walking on it and the first to be immersed in that water followingg the angel would be healed. Instead hearing the man's explanation Y'shua did more than the man expected, he simply told him to pick up his bed and walk. This caused quite a stir among the Pharisees because it was the Sabbath day and the wanted to know who did this healing. Later when Y'shua met him again he warned him to sin no more or something even worse might happen to him. Imagine, something worse than being crippled for 38 years! This unnamed man did return to the Pharisees to tell them who had healed him and we learn that Y'shua uses this incident to demonstrate his authority from Heaven. The man however didn't do what so many of us do today, he didn't question the authority of Y'shua, he did as he was told and followed the instructions.

In John 8 we have the familiar lesson of the woman accused of adultery, but what so many modern Christian sermons leave out (because they don't study) is the real people in this lesson who are sinning are the Pharisees! That's right, they bring a woman caught in the act of adultery to Y'shua and make the statement that according to the law of Moses she must be stoned. according to Deuteronomy 22:22, both the man and the woman must be brought to trial and if they are indeed guilty both offenders were to be killed to prevent evil in the land. Yes, the pharisees only brought the woman, their first sin, then they lied and twisted the scripture to imply only the woman is to be killed, their second sin. Next they bore false witness against the woman because adultery is the only command that requires 2 people to commit, their third sin. Now as Y'shua outwits the Pharisees and tells them let the one without sin through the first stone; he has thePharisees caught in their own trap. Since there are not two or more witnesses to testify, the woman can not be found guilty, Y'shua judges her innocent but he then gives her this stern warning, "Go, and sin no more."

Since we now understand that sin is a choice we know it is entirely possible to live our lives according to the instructions that our Creator gave to us. Those instructions are not so foreign to us that we need to search for them. Deuteronomy 30 beginning in verse 12 reminds us that the instructions are not in Heaven or across the ocean so we need to send someone to retrieve them, they are close to us.! John 5:3 reminds us the instructions are not burdensome, Matthew 11:30 Y'shua said his yoke is easy and his burden light. This list of passages for humans to be able to follow God's instructions is very long, and the list of warnings for failing to follow those instructions is long as well.

Even Paul makes the statement in Romans 6 that we are no longer a slave to sin, but instead a slave to righteousness. We have the choice of masters, we can choose Satan or we can choose our Creator, do we follow the Creator or the created? Y'shua understands the struggle that is in our hearts, most of us want to follow God's instructions but have been taught, even trained to be sinners. To believe Y'shua and choose not to sin we must use the same definition he would use and then recognize sin when we see it and the best way to do that is to follow God's instructions to the best of our ability. For the average person, the easiest way to understand the instructions is to remember the 10 commandments. The rest of the instructions in the Bible (with the exception of the Tabernacle, temple and priests which served in them) are all derived from these first 10 matters given at Mount Sinai. Y'shua makes it very clear and quite easy for us to follow his commands to go and sin no more, the choice is ours to make.

Today there are many Christian denominations which teach that because of the death burial and resurrection of Y'shua we are no longer "under the law." Different denominations get this from parts of different verses and twist them to suit their individual agendas. This doctrine of disobedience fails to maintain any resemblance of Biblical Authority. An analogy would be this, a football team scores 17 points during a game but when asked if the won the game, they only answer "we scored 17 points." When they concentrate on only their score they are trying to avoid the real question, "Did you win?" "We scored 17 points!" To be honest, we were never "under the law" as some people like to say. The choice has always been ours, Adam chose to sin, Jonah chose to sin, we can choose to sin.

By twisting the words from Paul's letters, some Bible teachers have convinced far too many people that they no longer need to follow God's instructions. Some of these denominations have their own instructions which they follow and Matthew 5:19 the words of Y'shua tell us that the people who choose not to follow God's instructions and teach others to be disobedient will suffer. Look around your community, do you see people in leadership positions at their churches suffering any physical ailments? diabetes, high blood pressure, heart disease or cancer are just a few of the manifestations in our physical world which could possibly be avoided if these people would repent and sin no more, or something worse might happen to them. We watch the television evangelist who seem to be so popular and on top of the world trying to convince people to send them money. They live in large houses and drive expensive cars only to suffer humiliation, divorce, bankruptcy or worse.

Consider the people we watch on television, the movies or who play professional sports. When these celebrities humble themselves and give god the glory for their talent the world tries to persecute them, but even when their career in the spotlight is over most of them have a successful future. Compare that to the superstars who live as there is no God, what do we see? addiction, disease, divorce humiliation. Now look around your own community again, what do you see? people who may not be attending church regularly but who are humbly feeding the hungry, helping the widows, mentoring the fatherless or motherless, how is their health and their attitude? sadly, probably better than most preachers. The blessing and the curses we read about in Deuteronomy 27 are still enforced from Heaven today if we would open our eyes and look around. We have the ability to observe people and how they live, not the big houses or the fancy clothes, but their attitude; are they happy in their wealth? are they content in their poverty? are they doing what their Creator is asking them to do? Are they using the skills God knit into their souls while they were in their mothers womb to benefit the people around them? The most content people, whether they go to church or not, whether even know who Y'shua is or not are following God's instructions simply by design. They have found their life is easier when they do the things they are designed to do. Most of them can't explain why they do what they do they just continue to benefit the people around them because it makes them happy while the people who try to benefit only themselves are miserable.

Don't get these blessings and curses confused with why bad things happen to good people. Remember Job, a righteous man who trusts God and whom God trusted explicitly in the hands of Satan. Because of their relationship God knew He could trust Job to remain faithful and defeat Satan. Sometimes what we see as something bad our Creator is using to display faith to someone who needs to see it. The way with which we remain faithful during an illness or some other trial is God answering our prayer that another is shown a way to have faith in God. That might sound backwards but it is a Biblically sound observation of the way our Creator does things. Satan's accusation of "The only reason they are faithful is because of what you give them" could only be false when proven that people come to have faith in their Creator because of adversity. If God was only a "sugar daddy" and we were only following him as long as things were going well then Satan's statement found in Job would be true but because people do see how believers respond to difficult situations and become themselves believers we know Satan's statement is false. We should stop asking why bad things happen to good people and instead ask "Who is our creator trying to reach through this situation?"

Many people who try to justify a lifestyle of sin seem to enjoy harassing those who are following God's instructions. They accusation is works won't get you into Heaven, but forget that faith without works is dead according to James chapter 2. Sometimes they will use the phrase "you're being legalistic," in a negative tone but the truth is they are being disobedient, and disobedience is the vehicle that brought death and the curses into creation with Adam and Eve. When pressed to give a reason for their disobedience the answer is typically one of two responses, the law's been abolished or Jesus fulfilled the law so I don't have to. There are other similar responses but they are equal to the same these. Ok let' follow their logic; first the law's been abolished, so we can rob, kill, pillage and do whatever we want to now because there is no law? the blank stare means the person you're speaking with never equated the 10 commandments with the rest of the law. Their surprised "oh, no we can't do that!" brings my next question; "Why?" When they try to explain that the 10 commandments still stand but the rest of the law doesn't they become trapped in their own dilemma. One either believe the Bible or they don't, If you try to believe only the parts you choose to believe that is when you fail to believe the bible and begin to go your own way. When you begin to treat the Bible as a list of good ides to choose from you alienate Biblical Authority and replace it with you. You become your own authority!

Think back to the exodus, the last plague that God used to deliver the people from Pharaoh was the death of the first born. The Egyptians at that time worshipped Pharaoh ad a god; a man worshipped as a god leads to self worship and that is why our Creator used this last plague to destroy that concept. We are no different today when we use our Bibles as nothing more than a list of good ideas to choose from we begin the process of self worship because we abandon any supreme authority. Then the question becomes who has the better list? which things do we keep and what do we throw out? God has already made it clear in Deuteronomy we are not to add to or remove any of His instructions, His list is perfect just the way it is.

The other phrase that "Because Jesus kept the law perfectly so I don't need to" is a bit more complicated. 1 Peter 2:21–22 reads that Y'shua is our example and we are to follow in his footsteps because he did not sin and no deceitful words came from his mouth. IN chapter 3 of Paul's letter to the Philippians he writes that we should press on to be perfect to be more like Y'shua. So if he was ale to keep the law and we are to be more like him how should that excuse us from being obedient? it doesn't. If we are to be more like Y'shua maybe we should do the things he did such as follow the Father's instructions, eat the things he ate, rest on the Sabbath, are you getting the idea? Trying to argue logically against an illogical statement is—well, illogical. Instead change the course of the conversation, challenge the person with where in the Bible did you read that? (they didn't read it in the Bible because it isn't there.) What this dialog reduces to is people have believed the lies of their fathers as it reds in Jeremiah 16:19. They have been trained to sin.

Paul writes we do not fight against flesh and blood but against principalities, Ephesians 6:12. He is right we battle against the spirits of false doctrine and against ignorance. We battle against the spirit of deceit and the spirit of evil. often this battle is within ourself and sometimes it is with others but we battle and when our ammunition is Biblical Authority we have the ultimate weapon. Remember that in spiritual battles just like in physical battles people get hurt, feeling get hurt, and sometimes relationships fall apart. Use your ammunition wisely, some people need a soft touch while others need a far more direct "in your face" approach. Allow the Holy Spirit to guide you and when you don't have any words—don't speak but when you are given the words speak only what you are given.

When Y'shua said "Go and sin no more," he spoke of repentance, turning your entire life around to live the way we are all designed by our Creator to live. Following God's instructions brings the promise of blessings which include a long, happy, productive, successful life. Using our Bible as a kind of instruction manual teaches us how to live as individuals, as a family, as a community and as a nation. This is looking forward to the future, there are people who are discovering how they can improve their lives everyday by doing nothing more than following God's instructions. The media seems to report weekly about the death of the church because so many mainstream religions are loosing membership but drive down most roads and you will se small yard signs welcoming people to a house fellowship or a Bible study. There is a type of revival in the world today but the large denominational churches are not part of it and in fact they are trying to stop it. Still thousands of people each month according to the media reports are leaving the churches, they are repenting and they are meeting with like minded believer who are trying their best to follow God's instructions and sin no more.

CHAPTER 10

THIS NEXT CONTRADICTION will make the church lady stand up and shout "Now isn't that special!" That reference to the old Saturday Night Live skit in which Dana Carvey portrays a "church lady" who would sometimes offer commentary or interview celebrities from the perceived viewpoint of the church should give a hint to the topic. Are we the example to the world that we should be? Deuteronomy 19:4–5 read that if we obey His voice and follow His instructions we will be a nation of priests, an example to the world. For the people who think this only applies to the Hebrew bloodline we need to remember that in Exodus 12 there is only one law, one set of instructions given for the direct descendants of Abraham and those who choose to join with them and call the God of Abraham their own God. Paul uses the word adoption, we are adopted by our Creator. Jeremiah repeats that if we hear His voice and obey His instructions He will be our God and we will be His people. Just as with any adoption we receive the family name, 2 Chronicles 7; 14 begins, If my people who are called by my name; and that name is הוהי. However you wish to pronounce it (or not) those four Hebrew letters become part of us.

However we understand the concept, it is the same, when we accept that the Creator of the universe is the God of Abraham, we then become His representative. The way we represent our Creator displays what we think of Him. When we act as if following His instructions is a burden (and that isn't in the Bible) the people around us sense our negative feeling to our God. When we degrade someone (James 3; 9) the people around us again see a negative reaction to our Creator. On the other hand when we are in the center of what others might see as a negative situation but we keep our faith and continue to praise God, then others see a positive feeling displayed in a bad situation and that is what draws people closer to God. When we display a judgmental type of personality (as the church lady does) the people around us know that is a very negative attitude and have no desire to be a part of it, except maybe to laugh at the hypocrisy and sadness of it.

So where in the Bible do we get the idea that we can display this sort of behavior? we are never given permission in the Bible to act in a self righteous way. Paul writes that when we are following the Holy Spirit we will display what he calls the fruit of the spirit which are; love, joy, peace, patience, kindness, goodness,

faithfulness, gentleness and self-control and can be found in Galatians 5:22–23. With this in mind which spirit are we following if we display self righteousness? certainly not the Holy Spirit of our Creator! What about when we display pride or arrogance? these are not products of the Holy Spirit either. Of course we can be proud of our children when they accomplish a difficult task and boast about how God helped them to achieve a goal but remember that is not self serving, it is glorifying our Creator. We need to be mindful of the intent of the person who is speaking or acting and not base our judgement on their actions alone.

Remaining with the fruit metaphor, even though we can not put the fruit back on the tree, if we are quick enough to pick it up as soon as it falls or better yet catch it on the way down; we have the ability to prevent that fruit from being damaged. That is to say; if we respond fast enough to correct a situation we can intercede and possibly stop someone from making a mistake. Just as God place Adam in the garden to tend and cultivate it we have the responsibility to watch out for those around us. We tend a different kind of garden, cultivating positive responses and actions from the people around us by displaying positive and responsible actions ourselves. Never being selfish or greedy but instead using the skills our Creator gives us to benefit the people around us first and benefitting ourselves secondary because of our actions. We all know the phrase "You have to spend money to make money," well; we need to be a benefit to others to benefit ourselves.

When we follow God's instructions and use the skills He gives us to help the people around us, we get the feeling of satisfaction. We receive a greater benefit from putting others first, that may sound backward but it is the way we are designed by our Creator. There are some people in the world who will try to selfishly take advantage of any situation they can: that is their problem, leave it alone. Don't allow yourself to become absorbed into that world. They will need to answer for themselves but when you choose to do what is right, you will be rewarded. The self righteous, overreaching stereotypes such as the church lady reveal which spirit they are following when you understand what to watch for. The old saying "Do as I say not as I do," is abundant in the modern churches today. Too many people are willing to set standards for others but fail to maintain those same standards on their own and then wonder why they have empty pews on Sunday mornings. Hypocrisy, jealousy, arrogance and pride are just a few of the attitudes which lead to loneliness. nobody wants to be around people who display these actions.

Too often today we witness churches condemn certain actions while refusing to display any act of kindness to the very people they are condemning. There is the opposite extreme as well when churches go out of their way to accept anybody doing anything without holding anyone responsible. Which group is following the Holy Spirit and following the instructions given by our Creator? Neither of them! Yes we do have the ability and the responsibility to condemn certain actions that oppose Scripture. We also have the responsibility to display how to follow God's instructions and be the example and the witness to the rest of the world. When we simply exclude someone for their actions without offering the correct example and displaying the appropriate love for our neighbor then we are failing to follow the example that Y'shua displayed for us while he was here on earth. We also fail to follow that example when we accept everything and anything that people want to do.

Any group of people who choose to worship together are free to have rules which govern their social structure. As a group they can decide that a divorced person can not teach Sunday School or sing in the choir but we can not base that decision on the Bible because there are provisions in the Bible for divorce. The reason given for that decision is simply this social group doesn't allow divorced persons to participate in leading worship in any way. Of course we can replace many different actions here for the example of divorce: adultery, homosexuality, prior imprisonment or whatever the situation may be. The problem is there are many people hiding behind the veil of the church and forcing their will on others. They proclaim that certain actions are sin when they are not and fail to confront sin when it it in front of them; but can not see they, themselves are sinning when they add to or subtract from the words of God. Some of these churches are content to allow anyone to sit in a service but how long before these people leave because they are forever being chastised? When does the forgiveness and inclusion become part of the ministry? The Bible teaches us that restoration is a vey important concept, from restoring the earth to it's original glory to restoring relationships, we have a responsibility to be the example. Continued punishment once someone has repented is no more than inflicting hell on earth to each other. We were not created for and were never given the authority to torment each other this way. Instead we are to show compassion and love for each other and do our best to demonstrate how to follow the instructions God gives us.

Ezekiel 18 describes this exactly, we read that when someone who has been doing evil repents and does what is righteous, none of their wickedness will be mentioned. If our Creator is wiling to say "we will never speak of these thing again," why do we continue to admonish someone for their past once they have repented? Of course if there is no repentance there can be no forgiveness and forgiveness is a funny thing in the modern Christian church. I have personally witnessed the immediate forgiveness of a church leader who was caught in a very compromising situation and this person never repented and began to correct the situation. This same church however because the situation led to a divorce wouldn't allow the spouse (who had done nothing wrong) to even sing in the choir. The double standards in these circumstances need to stop if the church has a desire to follow Biblical Authority. Again Ezekiel 18 continues to teach us that if a righteous person begins to do what is wicked none of their righteous acts will be mentioned. Yes, we can forgive someone for their actions but we are not required to continually subject ourselves to their wickedness.

There is not a fine line that we walk but it is a narrow road. Our goal is to display the kindness to others that God offers to us. We need to be loving while maintaining the integrity of Scripture. This is not difficult but it can be confusing if we try to inject our own cultural traditions and church doctrines into God's instructions. We should try to separate our tradition, doctrine and rituals from the authority of the Bible. Biblical Authority should always be placed above any church doctrine or tradition. Every effort should be made to reduce the appearance of hypocrisy in our churches and in our personal lives. We choose to live by God's Biblical Authority or by our own authority. Whenever we try to justify our actions in an attempt to have the Bible match something we think or do we fail to uphold Biblical Authority and have replaced it with our own. Isaiah 64 reminds us that we are the clay and the Father is the potter. We are the ones being shaped and perfected God is the one who changes us to what He would have us become. We do not have the luxury of changing our Creator to make Him what we think He should be.

When we look at the Bible as a list of good ideas to choose from, we eliminate the Biblical authority and replace it with our own. We may like the "thou shall not kill" but think it is perfectly acceptable to omit a few details while trying to earn a few dollars. Leviticus 19 directs us to be sure to use honest weights and measures when buying and selling, is that something we are willing to give up? The instructions we have are designed so that everyone is treated fairly, not everyone is exactly equal in their finances but we are required to treat the rich and poor exactly alike. That doesn't mean we should allow someone to take advantage of our good will but it does mean that simply because someone may not have the resources that another has that we degrade them in any way. I know people who proudly proclaim that when they became a Christian they told God they would do this or that. Here is a radical idea; tell God that you agree to do the best you can at following His instructions, all of them that apply to you. That way you will never be viewed as or laughed at for being the hypocritical Church lady.

CHAPTER 11

MANY MODERN CHRISTIANS have a real desire to be disciples but they don't really understand what a disciple is or know how to reach their goal. There are books and programmed Bible studies which attempt to provide the information to turn someone into a disciple but if you have a true heart for it and really want to become a disciple of Y'shua, then read and understand what he teaches. Don't worry about the miracles yet, concentrate on the teaching.

Matthew chapters five, six, and seven are basic training for being a disciple. While many Bibles refer to these chapters as the sermon on the mount, careful reading reveals the first twelve were the only ones who were there to hear these instructions. When Y'shua began with what we have named the beatitudes, he began with "blessed are the poor in spirit," and a real disciple would know that he was repeating something that was recorded in Isaiah 66. In fact everything that Y'shua is teaching can be found in the Torah or the prophets. How does this help someone become a disciple? Easy, we know it is Y'shua speaking and who he is speaking to, (those he chose to be there) and we know who he is speaking about. This puts everything into the context so when we go back and study the passages he refers to we have even more context. The Bible defines itself, we don't need to interpret it because when we use it properly God's word stands on it's own foundation. Each passage when used in the context of self definition explains another lesson. There is no need to guess about what it means, the Bible itself reveals the meaning and the context if we take the time to study.

There are many useful tools we have today to help with this, from searchable digital programs on our computers to videos and reference books but the best reference book is the Bible. These tools help us quickly locate connected passages so that we are better able to understand the lesson we are glean from the word of our Creator. John 12 Y'shua said he is only able to speak what the Father has given him to speak. From this we should be able to read what he said and go back to the Torah or the prophets and find every lesson he was teaching. When Y'shua uses the phrase "It is written," we know we can go find where it is written. When he said "You have heard it said," then we know he is referring to something the religious leaders had instituted as law. Using the tools we have today makes it very easy to find the places where it is written.

With Matthew 5, 6, and 7 being disciple training camp, even though we only get the short details of what Y'shua is teaching, when we go back int what we call the Old Testament to find the places where it is written we gain the context and further understanding. This can be intensive study but well worth the effort if we choose to become true disciples. Having witnessed some amazingly miraculous things I am certain that when we truly have a working knowledge of what being a disciple is and an understanding of how to use the power and authority which comes with it, the miracles we read about on the pages of the Bible are possible in our presence. A miracle is conformation from Heaven that the person speaking has the authority from the Almighty to do something. Not everyone heals, not everyone raises the dead, true miracles don't need to be that dramatic. I met a gentleman who had a sever stroke and while attending a support group he witnessed others in far worse condition than he was in. His short almost unintentional prayer was; "Please God don't let me wind up like what I'm seeing." After some intense physical therapy, perseverance and determination, today to see him you wouldn't know he had ever been sick a day in his life. Yet he wasn't convinced that God even existed let alone answered his prayer because he wanted to see a miracle. When I said "you are the miracle!" he replied, "No, a real miracle, like the sea parting." I explained to him that the sea of sickness did part for him and he walked through it. I heard months later that he did finally see that he was the miracle and had accepted that his Creator did indeed bring him back to where he was before his stroke. Unfortunately, we often don't see the miracles in front of us because we are too busy looking for the miracles other places.

Becoming a disciple requires training and conditioning. Just as soldiers prepare for battle disciples must prepare for a different kind of battle. In Matthew 16 Y'shua tells his disciples if they want to follow him pick up a cross. Becoming a disciple costs more than what some want to pay, you will lose some of your friends, some of your family and all of your past. Becoming a disciple will cost you change. Your lifestyle will change, your friends will change, everything about you will change. Even if you thought you were a good person, when you become a disciple you will become the person your Creator designed you to be. Even if you consider yourself a Christian now, once you understand what a disciple is; you will change.

You will be able to recognize evil, unholy spirits, demon, and devils. you will know them by the look in the eyes of the ones who follow them, you will know them by the stench of the oder they radiate. You will no longer be able to remain silent when you hear false teaching because becoming a disciple means that you give yourself completely to your Creator. Just as the Spirit of the Creator put on Odeon and wore him like a coat in Judges 6, when you become a willing participant in this spiritual battle God will use you for His benefit. Becoming a disciple isn't all fun and games, it isn't just teaching Sunday School and serving turkey at Thanksgiving. You are already designed with everything it takes to become a disciple but God does not force it onto you. You must be willing, you must accept the job and then study for it. Learn to place Biblical Authority above all else, allow God to work through you and use you and never compromise Biblical foundations. Yes there is far more to becoming a disciple than reading through the gospel of John. Becoming a disciple may mean that cross you are carrying will be used as your execution stake. If you are not willing to follow Y'shua's example as Peter writes in 1 Peter 2 and wash someones dirty feet or sweep the floor or put the chairs away; how will you be able to serve the widows and the orphans? How will you feed the hungry? How will you give a drink to the thirsty? If you can't do that how will you run the race until you reach the end as Paul writes? Training, conditioning and faith; this is what Y'shua was teaching in Matthew 5, 6, and 7.

Is it worth the price? Absolutely! Look at John, he was beaten, and by some accounts boiled alive in oil but he was rewarded with seeing Y'shua while he was exiled on the island of Patmos. I'm certain there are many examples of people since, we see many people rewarded for their faith. I know I have been rewarded on this earth when I think about the things I have been able to accomplish and when I look at my family. I like to imagine each of us in some way has been able to receive some type of reward as conformation from Heaven that God is working in the lives of everyone. His way of whispering in our ear,"here I am, remember me? See what I have done for you?" Some of us recognize it and cling to it and some of us reject it. When we maintain Biblical Authority without compromise we are hated by those who reject it. Choose the topic; evolution, homosexuality, divorce, the list is practically endless, there are those even within the church who reject the parts they don't agree with. Remember the Bible is not a list of good ideas to choose from, it is the words of our Creator; Don't murder is equally as important as don't steal. We are told to love the LORD our God with all of our heart, mind, soul, and strength, not just part of it. Some try to hold back a portion of their "all" but that doesn't work. God wants to be involved with every aspect of your life not just the big stuff. He cares about every decision you make and wants to be part of all of them. Yes, it is worth the price to be a disciple, being a disciple means you are connected to your Creator. What He wants you want, You love what He loves and you hate what He hates. That also means that those who love Him love you and those who hate Him hate you too.

How does our Creator respond to those who hate Him? It rains on the just and the unjust also (Matthew 5.) The same rain that causes the food to grow for the righteous falls on the food for the wicked, that is the example we follow. When someone hates you; love them enough to pray for them, ask God to send someone to witness to them that they will hear. On the other hand, when we love what the Father loves, we read throughout the Bible of blessings almost too numerous to count. John 13 lets us know that it isn't how many verses we can memorize, or how many hymns we know all the word to, it is our love; the way we treat each other that displays if we are a real disciple. Matthew 7 Y'shua said the false teachers will be known by their fruit, in other words what you see them do, their actions and the actions of those they teach. The same is true of the righteous, they will be known by their actions. God doesn't want to hear we love He wants to see that we love.

Becoming a disciple requires training because in our fallen world we are not conditioned to love. We have to actually work at love. Sure it is easy to say we love but to display that love does not come easy at first. When Adam and Eve were exiled from the garden the world changed, death, destruction, thorns, and all of the rest of the curses we know now overshadow what once was our perfect world. That is what makes the emotion of love so difficult to display, it almost goes against nature. When we only look at the physical world we see the death and destruction but if we take time to examine the spirit of this world we see our Creator still at work, still loving his creation. Loving it so much He was willing to do whatever He could to restore creation to what it should be and God begins with people. Adam and Eve sinned and now all of creation groans as we read in Romans 8, but because God chooses to love us enough to restore humanity, even creation will be restored to what it was designed to be. Once we recognize the Father's love for us we are then able to display that love. Johns first letter chapter 4 reads "We love because He first loved us;" our nature is not to love first but as a result of being loved.

The result of maintaining strict Biblical Authority is not legal adherence to God's instructions but instead using those instructions to display love for ourself and our neighbor. Each of the instructions we received through Moses teaches us how to love, don't put other gods in the face of the Creator, honor your parents, don't steal, be honest. Even the other instructions remind us to treat each other fairly, treat animals humanely, and continually praise the Creator for everything you have been blessed with.

Unfortunately today, some try to convince us that following our Creator's instructions is little more than legalism. These people view obedience to God as a bad thing. They try to choose which "rules" to follow but fail to understand they are replacing God's authority with their own. Nowhere in the Bible is it written if we follow God's instructions we are guaranteed a place in the Heaven but because we have allowed the Scripture to be twisted without regard to Biblical Authority the battle cry for the disobedient has become "You're being legalistic!" No, not legalistic, obedient.

Y'shua said in Matthew 5:17–19 that he did not come to do away with the law, in fact until Heaven and earth are remade perfect once again the law will remain and anyone who teaches differently will be least one the kingdom. Yes, being a disciple means being obedient, there is no way to follow the teacher and go your own way at the same time.

One of the most used arguments concerns the sacrifices, Daniel chapter 9 puts those worn out argument to bed when we maintain Biblical Authority. Gabriel was sent to Daniel to give him the answers to some of his questions. In verse 26 we read that the Messiah will be cut off but not for himself, then in verse 27 we learn that in the middle of the week there will be an event that will cause the sacrifices and the oblations to cease. There is one singular event in history that meet these criteria. The crucifixion certainly caused the Messiah to be cut off but not for himself, he died as the final lasting sacrifice. This one event that caused the sacrifices to cease, to no longer be necessary. The blood of a sacrifice is never wasted, and the blood of Y'shua paid the cost of our death penalty that was owed to our Creator. Although the Pharisees didn't understand what was happening at the time they attempted to continue with the sacrifices until the destruction of the temple. One single event in history was given to Daniel by Gabriel (Who stands in the presence of God, Luke 1:19) but no one understood what it meant until after it happened. There are more layers of this same prophecy that we will not understand until another event makes them clear.

Being a disciple means more than going to church every Sunday morning, it means studying to show yourself approved, (2 Timothy) it means following the example that we have been given in Y'shua as Peter wrote in his first letter 2:21. Being a disciple isn't glamorous, isn't fashionable and certainly isn't always easy but is is worth the effort. Following the example that Y'shua gives us brings comfort when we hurt, healing when we're sick, hope when things like dark and more blessings than we could ever imagine. Maybe that's where we get the saying that anything worthwhile is never easy.

CHAPTER 12

We view time as a restrictive concept. Sixty seconds in a minute, sixty minutes in an hour. Twenty four hours in a day and 365 days in a year. A definite number of carefully calculated segments, each precisely fitting into what we have come to know as time. Even the Almighty Creator Himself designed periods of light and darkness that cycle before the sun, moon, and stars were created. Genesis 1 teaches that the light which God created on day one was different than the sunlight we witness today. This "God—light" which was created half way through the first day of creation reveals that God determined how long a day would be three days before the sun was created. This same God—light will once again be our light after Heaven and earth are remade perfect once again. Revelation 21:23 reads that we will not need the sun or the moon because the lamb will be our light, continuing the cycle of light and dark for eternity.

Solomon writes in Ecclesiastes, there is a season for everything, a time to plant and a time to harvest. A time to fight and a time for peace, a time to live and a time to die, and the list goes on. In Genesis 6 God limits our time in this life on earth to one hundred twenty years. With all of the witnesses to time in the Bible, why have we been trained to consider that time is a limit to be afraid of? The Bible reveals cycles, not limits, changes certainly but never in a negative connotation. Each cycle brings into play a new and exciting period of growth and understanding. Since creation, creation has experienced several periods in which the Creator has woven onto the fabric of His creation. We read about the flood, how Abram was chosen to be the father of a nation, the time the Hebrews were in Egypt, the exodus, and numerous other periods throughout history. Every one of these points on our historical timeline is part of a seamless transition within creation.

The flood, the most cataclysmic event in history appears to have occurred at precisely the right time in the exact order it should have because our Creator, the great maestro was conducting his creation to perform the crescendo which would transition this broken world into a time of rebirth. This cycle will happen at least twice again in the future. Once just prior to the arrival of the reigning Messiah during what most people would think of as the tribulation and then again at the end of the Messiah's millennial reign during the final war with evil. Each time creation is reborn into another period in the attempt to recover as many lost souls as possible before both Heaven and earth are shaken apart completely and our Almighty Creator makes them perfect once again, this time his perfect creation will last forever.

Too many people want to get trapped into the argument about the times we are living in. Every generation has been concerned with this, it is quite possible that during the Greek occupation of Israel the Maccabee's were wondering if they would see the coming of the Messiah to free them from their oppressor. We read in 1 Samuel 8, God tells Samuel they have not rejected him but the people have rejected God as their king, repeating the cycle to a somewhat lesser degree than just prior to the flood when people were doing what was right in their own eyes. In John chapter 1 we read the people asked John the Baptist if he was "the" prophet. this refers to Deuteronomy 18:15 when God tells Moses he will raise a prophet from among the people who will do greater things than even Moses did. This question also implies that the people of that time were searching for that prophet. By asking this question we can consider they were thinking or at east hoping that God would be sending this person soon, they were watching and waiting for him. Unfortunately, they asked the wrong person, John would answer he was not even worthy to untie his sandals. No one asks Y'shua if he was "the prophet," but in Matthew 8 and Mark 5 we learn that the demons know who Y'shua is. The two possessed men called him by name and begged him not to send them back, they knew his power and his authority and yet the people of that era couldn't identify him. They were looking for something different that God was supplying for that time.

We get caught today much the same way, we are looking for something other than what God is giving us. Often we will not be able to recognize that a prophecy has occurred util another event has taken place that put it into context. The people who lived during the first century were not looking for an event to cause the sacrifices to cease as Daniel chapter 9 describes. These people were looking for something larger, some great miracle to end their immediate suffering. They wanted someone who would lead a great army and end Roman occupation, what they got was someone who would tell them they needed to follow the

Creator's instructions and stop trying to do things their own way. Y'shua's primary message was for us to stop trying to live under our own authority and allow God to be our authority, to do things His way not our way. That message is exactly as popular today as it was then, people want to persecute the messenger displaying again the Biblical cycle we call time.

There are many who proclaim we live in the end times or the end of the age, maybe we do but it is still just a transition into another period. There is a fascination about when and how the next great tribulation will occur. Many people study it hoping to find specific date on which it will begin. Others look for the date and time to expect the reigning Messiah to show up. Some might even dread the idea of the next cycle approaching. Each of these groups have the same thing in common, they are looking for something they will only know when it happens. Throughout the Bible we are told to watch for things, the first sliver of the new moon to begin the new mont, when the barley is beginning to ripen in the spring and one of the most misunderstood is what is known as the counting of the omer, that 50 days between the Feast of first Fruits and Shavuot or Pentecost. When we are instructed to watch and be observant it is because we are being trained to be ready. Anyone can count to the fiftieth day after an event but why should we pay particularly close attention to these fifty days? Because we count down to something better, continuously watching, waiting, anticipating, searching to see what would happen that we would recognize. When we recognize something we will have a reference point to look back at an event in the past and see exactly when some prophecy was completed.

Historically, the celebration of Shavuot was to commemorate the giving of the ten commandments at Mount

Sinai. Deuteronomy 16:16 instructs that all men go to the place that God would choose (eventually, Jerusalem) to offer his tribute to God. If you have ever wondered why the list of people represented in Acts chapter 2 includes so many different groups? they were obeying the Torah and going to Jerusalem as they were instructed. They were there for the feast of weeks, Shavuot, what we call Pentecost today. The appointed time that God chose to give the ten commandments when He spoke directly to the people would be the same Heavenly date God chose to anoint people with the Holy Spirit. When we Maintain Biblical Authority we learn that our Creator in His infinite wisdom chose the same day to speak to his people, maybe in differing ways but He did not abandon His appointed time and the people who were there received a blessing they were not expecting. God doesn't use time as a limit for us He uses cycles to demonstrate to us His power, His glory, and His authority.

We live in a physical universe, that means we are confines to when we live. That may sound confusing but it really isn't Being confined doesn't mean we are limited, although we can't time travel into the past or the future, we remember and study the past. We have the ability to look back and carefully connect events and people. We also have the ability and the instructions to look to the future, to be ready for something, to watch so that we will recognize an event and be able to connect it with prophecy. We are confined to living in the present, we can not go back a re-do even a second ago but we can look forward to the future. We have hope, we have the opportunity to make our future better than our past.

The age or era we live in is only another cycle which our Creator uses to transition from lesson to another as He orchestrates His universe in a symphony of reconstruction. Everything God does is preparing His creation to be remade perfect once again, just like is was in Genesis when He said it was very good. We can't live in the past or visit the future but we can learn from the past to make our future better while we live in the present. When we can retrain ourselves to think of time differently, not as limited segments of a day or week but as unlimited cycles of opportunity, we can begin to understand time from a Biblical viewing begin using time the way our Creator intended. God gives us six days to work, he doesn't limit what we can do in those six days, but on the seventh day we rest.

On the seventh day we recharge the batteries, a mini vacation on day each week. Without getting technical about what is work and how to rest, I will say this, each person and each family is different. Everyone must decide on their own how they will rest. I have heard argument about everything and some are just ridiculous, acts of compassion are not necessarily work. Changing a baby diaper needs to be done and so does feeding a child. Certainly a family with young children will observe that day of rest differently than an older couple or a singe person, there are different instructions fro our Creator concerning these things as well. this is not a one size fits all uniform. Someone who owns animals needs to care for them. The sick still need care as well. Yet on the seventh day, we have been given the chance to slow down, relax, and allow our bodies and our minds to get invigorated.

Learning to use time the way our Creator intended for us to use it may seem odd at first when we still live in this world where we need to be at work or school on time. When there are certain deadlines to meet or the we think time is running out. Look around you and see what God did in just six days, He isn't asking us to accomplish any-thing at all like that; He is only asking for some help to keep things going. To use your skills to help someone else, to improve your life by helping to improve someone else life. When we can learn to do that, we have all the time in the world.

CHAPTER 13

When we Maintain Biblical Authority there are some traditions that we naturally begin to question. We have been trained that we need to accept the Holy Spirit in our hearts, or we need to accept Jesus int our heart. Neither of these phrases can be found in the Bible, the closest to it is Paul's letter to the Romans. In chapter 10 he writes that if we confess with our mouth and believe in our heart that Y'shua was raised from the dead we will (at some point in the future) be saved. That isn't accepting into anything but that is what some major denominations are teaching. Traditions can be good or bad, fireworks on independence day for most are enjoyable but for some of those who have seen war first hand, they are difficult to deal with. There are some traditions in our churches which are harmless such as standing to sing, however traditions which blatantly force others gods in the face of our Creator should be avoided no matter how much we enjoy them.

To be completely honest, here is where things may begin to get really difficult for some people. When we use Biblical Authority as our standard to measure many of the traditions used in our churches today those traditions simply will not stand up to the scrutiny. We often find the worship of other gods among these traditions which directly conflicts Deuteronomy 12 were we are instructed not to worship other gods or learn the way that other gods are worshiped and then try to worship our Creator in that way. He provides us with the way He chooses to be worshipped and says that everything else is an abomination; something so foul and despicable we are to avoid it and have nothing to do with it.

Some of these rituals conjure up images in our minds of witches standing around a black kettle stirring with their brooms and chanting. There are other traditional rituals which are not as easy to identify; they are the wolves in the sheep's clothing. While I would hope if a pastor wants to hold a worship service at sunrise on June 21 to sing praises to the sun for being in the sky on the longest day of the year no one in that congregation would follow and that pastor would be out of a job very quickly. Now change the date to any Easter Sunday and practically the entire congregation shows up at the sunrise service. None of the Gospel accounts concerning the resurrection mention sunrise. John 20 reads on the first day of the week while it was still dark; no sunrise here. Mark 16 reads early on the first day of the week, in a culture where days begin a t sundown when is early? Most probably in the evening.

When we stop forcing our way of thinking onto the pages of the Bible and allow it to guide us through the events being described we have a better idea of what really happened. But because we have been conditioned by many years of training we find it difficult to change the pictures in our mind. We have been taught to think we can magically count three days and three nights between Good Friday and Easter Sunday but we know that can't happen.

There is sufficient evidence to suggest the crucifixion was on a Wednesday, exactly the way Gabriel told Daniel it would be in Chapter 9. That then places the resurrection just before sundown on the Sabbath so when May gets to the tomb early while it's dark Y'shua isn't there.

I have been in many church services that will stand and sing the Doxology after receiving the offering. There isn't anything wrong with this tradition until some people think that it has become the eleventh commandment. When the preaching goes a little long and something needs to be left out and that happens to be the Doxology some people look like the roof will fall down on top of them. Some churches have a tradition where the children's Sunday School classes are brought in for the children's sermon. Again there is nothing wrong with this tradition, but remember it's tradition. The churches that have a choir every Sunday if the choir doesn't sing some people fell like something is missing, and there are some churches that when the pastor is on vacation the church is closed.

Our lives should not revolve around our traditions. If I ask most Christians today where the disciples were when the Holy Spirit arrived at Pentecost the most common answer is the upper room. Luke reports that there were over one hundred disciples at the time who were constantly in the Temple, specifically in an area known as Solomon's porch. Biblical Authority, making sure everything fits perfectly without forcing or twisting gives us the answers we search for, if we are willing to consider the answer.

Examine the last supper, some want to make it a Passover Seder which would be impossible for many reasons. First the Passover Seder wasn't utilized for almost two hundred years after the destruction of the Temple, Passover at the time of Y'shua was observed according to the Temple services given to David by the hand of God (1 Chronicles 28) a much different service than the seder we know today. Next we see in john 18 the Pharisees would not go into Pilate's judgement hall because they did not want to be defiled and unable to eat the passover. If Y'shua is the lamb of God he would not be able to be at his own supper, the lambs would be sacrificed the next day, this last supper is just that, the last meal before his crucifixion. The disciples were not having communion either and any reference to the last supper and communion should be avoided. there was no blessing the bread or the wine, careful reading reveals Y'shua offers the blessing that was handed down from the time of Abraham. The blessing is for the Almighty Creator who provides bread from the earth and is the creator of the fruit of the vine. There is no magical incantation to turn the bread into the body (something that no Judean would have suggested, it's only a representation) or the wine into the blood. We remember every time we offer the same blessing to our Creator praising Him for the blessing we receive.

Traditions are so embedded into our lives most of us don't realize we have them. Some people wake up every morning and do the same thing, the same way, in the same order, that is a tradition. Trying to change the order feels strange and almost foreign. Now imagine if we were to try and change the way you tie you shoe or even button your shirt, physical conditioning is as much a part of our traditions as the emotional or spiritual. retraining your mind and your body to accept something different is very similar to breaking a habit to overcoming an addiction. Of course if you are truly addicted to a tradition chances are you have been following an unholy spirit and need to repent. This is what makes dealing with church traditions difficult, there is the emotion of abandoning something we have been trained to do. Watch someone who stands up and takes a step, most people will always begin with the same foot forward each time that stand up from a chair. Now imagine a church congregation sleeping in on Easter Sunday morning, beginning their service at the regular time. Almost sounds disrespectful doesn't it, but who would they be disrespecting? The pagan sun god, but the Creator of the universe would be watching and smiling knowing that they are beginning to understand and act on that understanding.

Every time the young nation of Israel was exiled from the land can be traced back to a violation of the very first commandment: shoving some other god in the face of the Creator. Even King David was not immune from this, his hybrid religion (for lack of a better description) combined the Hebrew Temple Services with worship practices of the surrounding nations. This cycle of doing it God's way then doing it our way continued util God had appointed a time to correct the situation. Fast forward to the Greek occupation of Israel when the Maccabee stood up and shouted all the who are with Yehovah, follow me. That small band of faithful fighters were able to finally defeat the Greek army and some would add just in time for Roman occupation. History displays a cruel but fair punishment for disobedience to our Creator. After all it is His universe and we need to play by His rules. When God tells us to avoid something because it is bad for us, we may listen for a short time but we seem to always look at others who appear to be having so much fun without thinking their fun is very short lived. When we do things God's way He promises to give us a long, productive, happy, successful, and satisfying life.

The traditions we have inherited from our fathers are empty, Y'shua is recorded in Mark 7 as saying it is in vain you worship when you teach as doctrine the traditions of men. Vain means empty or worthless, when we hold onto worthless traditions we miss the real blessings our Creator wants to offer us. Those traditions are a wall that we put up between God and ourselves. Following His instructions help us break down that wall and slow us access to the power and the authority He wants us to have. John writes that Y'shua is the word, later he would add he is the way the truth and the light. Each of those adjective have been used to describe the Torah. Y'shua is the law, God's word in the flesh, following his example is following God's instructions.

There are other traditions in the churches that I encourage each person to examine on their own. Look at Halloween, Valentines Day, and even Christmas. I think you will be surprised at the discoveries you make when you use Biblical Authority as the standard to scrutinize these traditions. On the other hand you might be surprised at what you find when you really look into St. Patrick's Day also. Traditions have can evolve, when I was young Thanksgiving was a day to give thanks, eat a large meal and have all of the family at the table. (With the exception of the young ones at the "kid's table") Later Football began to be played on Thanksgiving day so the tradition evolved to eat earlier and watch football. The next step in the evolutionary process was for stores to open late int the evening and today we have people rushing through the meal while on their phones either watching a game or searching for coupons to be at the stores when they begin their sales in the afternoon. What are we thankful for? It's no longer having a loving God that supplies our needs or a family to support us when things are tough. Today we are thankful for the sales that saved us over 50%. Here is a radical thought; if you didn't buy anything you could have saved

100%. If you would have spent more time with the family you wouldn't miss them so much when they are no longer here and if you took the time to praise your Creator…well you get the idea.

examining our traditions with Biblical Authority reveals exactly how far removed we are from God. When we place more importance on some one or some thing than we do on our Creator, we are the ones who get out of sync with creation. The animas still praise Him, the stars and planets and even the rocks cry out but we who are supposed to be His greatest work too often choose to ignore Him and replace His instructions with worship we enjoy that waves other gods in His face.

Hopefully you are asking what can we do to avoid offending God. Begin with an honest examination of the traditions you choose to follow. Hold them up to The standard of Biblical Authority and see if they stand on their own merit. Sometimes you don't even need the Bible to do that, there are resources such as Christian encyclopedias which openly admit to some traditions as having their roots in pagan worship. when you slam the book and scream "That's not what it means to me!" Ask what it means to God, How does He see you worship? His way or your way?

CHAPTER 14

We live in world today where there is so much information readily available for use. There are old manuscripts and fragments of old writings which have been digitized and scanned onto searchable documents, many of which are translated into English. Archeologists have uncovered a treasure of artifacts that reveal exactly how those past civilizations lived. Science has finally again accepted that the Bible is a legitimate tool to be used in research. So with all of this information, how do we decide what is real and what is not? Biblical Authority. Does finding a piece of pottery with a cross on it in an ancient home in Israel mean there were Christians that used it? I can say with a definite and almost certain—maybe, but it is doubtful. during the persecution of the early followers of the way or the new sect of Jews as they were known, they had many enemies. The Pharisees encouraged the hunting down of these believer in Y'shua and "convincing" them to see the error of their way. Even though these early members of the church were being obedient to God they were not following the man made rules of the Pharisees and this was not acceptable to those who were in charge. So it is doubtful that they would have had anything to mark them as a follower of the way, including a cross on a piece of pottery.

There were many symbols used to decorate items throughout history, the swastika is a symbol which has been used in different forms since the time of Abraham. Today we think of it as a symbol of hate due to it's use in the National Socialist or the Natzi party. The fish is another symbol that is often associated with the early Christians and that symbol has been used by many different cultures but primarily those who were worshipping the fish god. The cross has been used by different cultures as well and because of it's unpleasant use during the time of Y'shua to crucify those opposed to Roman rule there is some reasonable speculation to it's use in the early church as a symbol for those who followed Y'shua. The Bible answers many questions but remains silent on some as well but remembering these were real people, living real lives and dealing with real problems helps put things into context. Think about it this way: would you even today use the symbol that represents the devise used to torture and kill your favorite teacher? Probably not, so finding a cross on a piece of pottery in Israel may not mean there were Christians who worshipped there.

There is practically an unlimited amount of speculation when any artifact is uncovered or when an old writing is discovered as to what it could mean. Depending on the viewpoint of the person who located the object there could be either positive or negative conjectures, the truth about the discovery may never truly be known. If we have enough information about something then we can examine it through the viewpoint of Biblical Authority and determine if it helps support the Biblical record of history. A small silver bell was located in Jerusalem and some rushed to judgement concerning who would have worn such an item and when. Finally the dust settled and enough information was collected for a reasonable person to consider this was probably form the clothing of a priest, possibly around the first century. There is no way to say who the priest was or what date the bell was made or when it was lost but after it was thoroughly examined there is still no way to be absolutely certain about who may have lost the object.

Sometimes we are fortunate enough to be blessed with enough information about a writing or an object that we know the details but not very often. Almost every week there is something new uncovered in Israel that connect the Hebrew people to the land they call home prior to anyone else living there. There is the now a fragment of what is being called a shopping list which was discovered in the Jericho region. This fragment gives just enough information for us to know there were Hebrew people in Israel before it was ever named Palestine. Equally exciting is the growing number of manuscripts of the book of Matthew written in Hebrew. While not to be overlooked are the many Greek versions of the Gospels that have had things added when compared to the very earliest known to exist. Each of these things support the Biblical timeline and the Biblical narrative.

This is not to say that the Bible as we know it today has no mistakes in it, certainly it does. There is a reference which Paul makes in 1 Corinthians 5 that he had written a letter to them before the letter we know as 1 Corinthians. Does this mean that 1 Corinthians is really 2 Corinthians? No, it means the first letter was probably lost or simply not preserved. Does it mean that we through out all of Paul's letters? No, it means we scrutinize them using the rest of the Bible. Are we going to ignore the Gospel writers for writing about the cock crowing when no chickens were kept in Jerusalem at the time they lived? Of course not, we research and digging into the language the culture and the history to find the reason for using this figure of speech. the cockcrow in Jerusalem would have not been a rooster but a familiar morning blowing of the shofar; the ram's horn or the horn from some kind of animal.

To grasp the context of the writers of the time we need to make every effort to understand not only the language but the culture and the history as well. That is where the other writings of the times are important. Not to prove the Bible but to give insight as to the way they used figures of speech, humor and even sarcasm. Y'shua uses sarcasm often if you know what to look for. When he was teaching the parable of Lazarus and the rich man he asks Lazarus your family have Moses and the prophets why would they believe someone who comes back from the dead? Most don't like to think of their "Jesus" as sarcastic but this really is sarcasm. The first to be resurrected using the line they won't believe someone back from the dead, God has a sense of humor.

There are writing which are not in the Bible and yet they describe Biblical accounts or offer insights into the people who lived during what we consider Bible times. Often given the title extra Biblical writings" these shouldn't be confused with the Apocrypha. The Apocrypha was removed from the Bible completely around 1895 by the British and Foreign Bible Society. This removal was based on several factors such as the Presbyterians wanting it excluded and other groups considering it uninspired but with printing cost to include it being the final decision for it's removal. The Apocryphal books hold a treasure trove of information. The Maccabees give us tremendous insight into the time between the last of the prophets and birth of John the Baptist. These writings as important as they are should not be used to prove or disprove any Biblical theory's we might consider. There is enough information in the Old Testament to verify everything that is in the New Testament. Using the Bible as it's own dictionary and encyclopedia, we can establish everything we need without the extra Biblical writings which are simply additional witnesses to what we should already know.

There are some questionable things in the Bible which we know were added later or changed outright by the Roman church influence. Y'shua's teaching in John 6, Matthew 26, Mark 14 and Luke 22 concerning eating his flesh is a good example, As I mentioned in an earlier chapter no Descendent of Abraham would even express eating human flesh or drinking blood because it is forbidden in the Torah. There is enough evidence to conclude that he is referring to himself as being represented in the blessing used with the bread which is: "Blessed are you Yehovah, our God, King of the Universe who brings forth bread form the earth." Y'shua teaches that he is the bread that the blessing is speaking of, this blessing that was handed down to Abraham by the righteous King Melchizedek. (Malki - Zedik מלכיצדיד) Abraham the instructed his family and his servants to continue with the blessing each time bread and wine are served. Y'shua is using what was a very familiar blessing to display the how Abraham saw his day and was glad (John 8.) The wine also represents blood and life, Y'shua is using this along with the wedding betrothal to represent a future event; the marriage supper of the lamb. In using these familiar aspects of everyday life Y'shua is able to bring Genesis and Revelation together with the fine teach about this being the last super. He perfectly combines everything from Abraham to the victory over death to display that he really is the beginning and the end, the Alpha and the Omega or as he would have said it the Aleph and the Tav.

Because there have been things changed by the church over throughout history we need to be very careful when we study. One more example is in Psalms 139 David declares we are fearfully and wonderfully made but then in just a few verses we read that were made imperfect. That statement contradicts that everything God makes is indeed very good doesn't it. This may be a bad translation or the editors wanted to impress their ideas into our understanding but the word imperfect here should be unformed. even before we take human shape, our Creator is working on us, we are not imperfect at birth but during the process from conception to form God shapes us into exactly what He chooses. I have heard this verse used to describe why God allows birth defects in infants but God if God forms us then we have no defects in His eyes. That might sound backward but it was Adam and Eve who brought imperfection into this world. God uses that imperfection to display HIs glory at a time He chooses. Sometimes through miraculous healing and sometimes to display the love and faith He wants us to display.

The information we have either contained in the Bible or in the archeological discoveries, the uncovered manuscripts and fragments of writings and even in the world of science all declare the glory of our Creator. All of creation is screaming that God is our ultimate Creator and our King but for some reason we humans still reject His word. Our arrogance appears to be that if the rocks choose to cry out then let Him be a God to them but we want to be our own god, go our own way and do things the way we want.

I know many people who proclaim they believe the Bible and yet they reject most of it. We often makes jokes about these kinds of people calling them "cafeteria Christians," they treat the Bible as a list of good ideas which they get to pick and choose from. This is the ultimate replacement theology, replacing God's instructions with our own ideas of what we want to do.

Today we have the tools to make understanding the Bible much easier, there are digitized manuscripts that are completely searchable. We have access to translation software that helps but is not a complete substitute for knowing the languages and the culture. There are concordances, lexicons, dictionary's and encyclopedias which all tell us the same thing; our traditions are far different than what the Bible record indicates. Nothing is now or ever was hidden, everything the Creator allows us to know was always within our grasp but most of us never reached for it. Most of us are content to believe what we hear from our parents, teacher, preachers, and even what we see on the Television and in the movies. Most of us were never taught to think critically about the Bible, to use Biblical Authority as our standard of measure. Instead we trusted the words of humans and have been confused, turned around and led away from our true Creator to believe in a fantasy that is only based on reality. When we question the fantasy, the information we uncover may not always be what we thought it should have been. Once we use the tools and resources at our disposal and see the facts we are then faced with the ultimate discussion: will I believe the Bible and what God is revealing to me or will I believe what I have been taught to believe by the people around me.

No one can answer that question for anyone else, this is a personal decision that each of us must make at some point in our lives. When we choose our prayer to be that God shows us the truth and teaches us to love the things He loves and to hate the things He hates, our lives will change. We discover new and exciting things about the Bible that we never expected and with each new discovery we ask ourself the same question; "Why didn't I see that before?" Once the truth becomes so obvious we don't realize how easy it is to be fooled and misled. Especially when we think we know the difference between good and bad, right and wrong, and righteousness and evil, we find our way of thinking about things and the way we see the world changes. The closer we get to our Creator our perspective of the world around us changes to be more like His. If you want people to see Y'shua reflected in your life you first need to be in his light and then close enough so that his reflection can be projected to everyone who see's you.

As we study to show that we are approved we gain that closeness and stand in that light. Using the information and the tools we have available enhances that study exponentially. Training ourselves to maintain Biblical Authority, to question and scrutinize the new theories and concepts about the world and even the Bible is not a difficult task. There will always be some around you that want to stand in your way, that will tell you "Well my preacher said..." But once you make the decision to live the way we are designed by our Creator to live those negative influences stop. This doesn't mean that we don't allow others to hold us accountable, the results of the things we do should always reveal Holy attributes. As Paul describes the fruit of the Holy Spirit is love, joy, peace, patience, gentleness, goodness, faith, Meekness, and self control. Certainly we will be angered with others who seen to have no concern with the results of their actions. Remember when Y'shua drove out the money changer from the Temple? What did he do just before he walks in and begins to chase out those money changers? He takes the time to braid a whip from small cords, Y'shua doesn't rush in but he calmly and deliberately takes time to see what he needed to do and then he drives out the people and the animals. I am in no way advocating violence but I am certainly in favor of taking the time to consider our actions when we are faced with witnessing actions that will result with the fruit of following an unholy spirit.

We should always be aware that the tools and information we use to discover the truth that is contained in the Bible are given to us by God. Deuteronomy 29:29 reads the secret things belong only to God but what He has given us belongs to us. Some people will accept the truth while others reject it. The book of Jude speaks about those people who reject the truth but they come to your meetings and meals to undermine the truth with their empty lies. Jude calls them spots or blemishes, clouds without water and trees without fruit. We should make an effort to find and associate with others who choose to live the way we are designed, people who choose to follow God's instructions, those who's actions reveal the fruit of the Holy Spirit. Fellowship with those who observe and celebrate the feasts that were established before Adam was created. Our Creator is continually revealing Himself to us in different ways, giving us more information, showing us that He is still in complete control of His universe. What we do with this information and how we reveal it to others displays our character and our determination to maintain Biblical Authority.

Information is power, is a phrase used quite often, and while it is true remember power can either build or destroy.

Our job is still to build the Kingdom of God and when we use the information He provides properly we are able to do exactly that. The end of Matthew is not just for missionaries, it is for us all; as we go through our daily routine, live in a way that teaches others to be disciples. Whether you are going to work, school or even the store, others see our actions and the result of the actions and they should want what we have, a trusting, faithful, solid relationship with our Creator.

CHAPTER 15

The Bible is often so specifically and exhaustingly detailed about some things while it seems to be exceedingly vague on others. Unfortunately we as humans sometimes forget that this vagueness is freedom, we are free to do good all of the time. If our actions will benefit another and glorify God we are completely free and also encouraged to do just that. We know that do not steal means not to take something we don't own without permission but late in the Torah it was necessary to be even more specific and we have the instructions about using just weights and measures and about moving boundary markers. Y'shua was being specific when asked what was the most important commandment. He told them to love God and love your neighbor then he said all of the commands are based on this. He was telling them that if they follow the instructions that God gave us through Moses those instructions would teach us how to love God and how to love our neighbor.

God is very detail oriented about the things we should not do but the vagueness concerns the things we are allowed to do. Maybe this is part of the reason for the confusion. God is not specific about how we display acts of compassion and kindness, we are free to express those things and more depending on the skills He gives to us. Doctors display kindness as they heal people, carpenters display compassion as they use their skills to build. We are free to be kind to each other depending on our own individual skills. there is no way that a one size fits all command could possibly cover all of the people who would ever live other than "love your neighbor," but we try to tear apart what we don't understand or claim that the law has been done away with.

Some of the most specific instructions concern food, what food is and what we should eat, or should not eat. The Bible is painstakingly so exact there an be no mistake about what food is but, we use a few obscure verses that have nothing to do with food, and twist them out of context to replace God's instructions with our own authority. I In the American culture we would not even think of eating a dog or cat or any of our pets but we are happy to have pork or shrimp. Other cultures consider these animals we think of as family delicacies and some prefer them more than beef. Maintaining Biblical Authority we are able to know exactly what we are designed to eat and what to avoid. I have been in churches that used Mark 7 to defend their ham and oyster dinners. Mark 7 and Matthew 15 give two perspectives about the same event. The Pharisees were upset about the way the disciples were eating bread without ritualistically washing their hands. Y'shua points out to everyone that following God's instructions is far more important than following our empty traditions but many people use theses passages to justify a ham sandwich.

Y'shua was speaking to a group of all Hebrew people, they knew what they were allowed to eat. The disciples asked him to clarify what he was teaching and he basically tells them that food (as defined by the Bible) doesn't make someone unholy, their actions are what makes someone Holy or unholy. If Y'shua was speaking to a group of gentiles this teaching would have been different. We are the ones who are grafted into Israel, (the people not the political nation) and we are the ones who are to hear God's voice and obey His commands to be called His people according to Jeremiah 7 and 24. What Y'shua is teaching isn't hard to understand or do but we don't like hearing that following God's instructions is better for us than replacing God's authority with our own authority.

Because I know we still need to clarify this discussion, lets look at Acts 10. Peter is given a vision while he was praying. All visions from the Holy Spirit are for a purpose, form Genesis to Revelation each time someone is given a vision we read about a specific purpose for it. This time Peters vision is about things he should not eat being offered to him and yet even in his vision he refuses to eat something he shouldn't. (this re-enforces Matthew 15 and Mark 7 being about something other than food) Peter being his usual self was confused about what his vision meant. Next we read about the three men sent by Cornelius because he want to meet with Peter. Somewhere between the time Peter had the vision and the time he went with the threw men to meet with Cornelius, Peter understood what the vision was about and he speaks directly to it in Acts 10:28; God had shown him, that he should not consider any "man" unclean. Peter's visit was not about food but about people.

The Bible may seem difficult to understand and some may try to convince us that we need to interpret the Bible but there is no need to interpret the Bible because it is self-defining. We read throughout the Bible about sin, but the actual definition isn't given until 1 John 3:4 which reads that sin is failing to obey God's instructions.

We should try to teach ourselves to study the Bible without using the filters that we have been taught from others, (no matter how well intentioned they were.) Read what is there on the pages without forcing our ideas and authority onto those pages and into the words. There is no need to add to what is there, some of the earlier Biblical editors have already added to it which added to our confusion.

The Bible is not a list of good ideas which we are allowed to choose from. The Bible is our instruction manual, it instructs us on an individual, family, community, and national level. The Bible is a living record of history, science, spirituality, and life. When we choose to reject it then we replace it with our own authority, each one doing what is right in their own eyes as the writer of Judges so aptly puts it. Being our own authority, going our own way and doing it my way usually doesn't work out well for us in the end. Eve did it her way when she was speaking to the serpent and look where we are today.

Maintaining Biblical Authority can be challenging, exciting, and yes, a little frightening at first but we discover there really are no contradictions in the Bible. Doing things God's way sometimes seems unnatural because we live in a fallen world. We witness the curses which Adam's rebellion brought into this world, disease, death, greed, lust, and deception are only a few of the unholy spirits we battle everyday. Our Creator gives us the ammunition to combat those forces through His instructions. He reveals to us hope, salvation, grace and life through his word. He really asks very little of us and that is to live the way we are designed to live by the Creator of the universe, so that it will go well with us all the days of our life.